Locate Disease Astrologically

Author

V. P. GOEL

Published by

Performonks Education and
Consulting Services LLP

First published in April 2016

Revised & Reprinted May 2024, Feb 2025

This is the Fifth revised edition.

ISBN: 978 - 81- 973347- 2 - 6

© V.P.Goel

Published by:

Performonks Education and Consulting Services LLP
44, Tatvam Villas, Sector 48, Sohna Road,
Gurugram, Haryana 122018
E-Mail: rashi@performonks.com

Preface

To be human is to battle disease and illness. That's why medical astrology is an important science and one that all astrology students are curious to learn.

Classical astrologers predict disease by reading planetary combinations. Those methods are useful too, but this book presents an alternative and novel approach through the use of divisional charts.

In fact, this book proves that when applied well, divisional charts can provide great insight into not just the timing of disease, but also which part of the body it originates in.

Let me explain how.

Locate the birth place of a disease.

Most doctors treat just the symptoms, and not the root cause of a disease. If you apply the methods in this book to pinpoint the exact place in the body or the organ where the disease took birth, you can seek treatment that addresses the root cause itself and not just the symptoms.

For example, in the book, I share the case of a person suffering from an eye problem. His problem was so severe that he was not even able to open his eyes, and had to resort to taking injections once a month.

On examination of the horoscope, it was revealed that his Venus was under heavy affliction - Venus was in Scorpio. Hence, the location of the disease was not the optical nerves, but the intestine. His condition improved dramatically once he started treatment for his intestine.

You can also adopt a preventive view.

These methods can predict when a particular disease will occur. Once the timing is known, the subject can take preventive measures ahead of time. This way, the severity of the disease may be reduced.

I have applied and tested the novel methods from this book across hundreds of horoscopes with high accuracy. I apply these methods across horoscopes in this book.

I sincerely hope that my fellow astrology students find this useful. I am also hopeful that bright young astrologers will further advance more research in this useful and interesting field of Medical Astrology.

V. P. Goel

vpgoel2019@gmail.com

Subscribe to my YouTube Channel:
"Saral Jyotish by VPGoel"

Books by the Author

हिंदी में	In English	In Russian
वर्ग कुंडलियों से सटीक फलित	Comprehensive Prediction by Divisional Charts	Comprehensive Prediction by Divisional Charts
योगिनी दशा से फलित	Snapshot Prediction using Yogini Dasha	Snapshot Prediction using Yogini Dasha
शोडाषोत्तरी दशा से फलित	Predict Through Shodashottary Dasha	
आयु रहस्य	Unravelling Puzzle of longevity	
	Predict Through Shasti Hayani Dasha	
	Locate Disease Astrologically	Locate Disease Astrologically
जैमिनी ज्योतिष से फलित	Predicting through Jaimini Astrology	Predicting through Jaimini Astrology
नवांश से फलित	Predict with Navamsha	Predict with Navamsha
सप्तांश से फलित	Predict with Saptamsha	Predict with Saptamsha
दशमांश से फलित	Predict with Dashamsha	Predict with Dashamsha
	Predict with Trishamsha	
सरल ज्योतिष 1	Saral Jyotish 1	Saral Jyotish 1
सरल ज्योतिष 1	Saral Jyotish 2	Saral Jyotish 2
सरल ज्योतिष 1	Saral Jyotish 3	Saral Jyotish 3
सरल ज्योतिष 1	Saral Jyotish 4	Saral Jyotish 4
सरल ज्योतिष 1	Saral Jyotish 5	
सरल ज्योतिष 1	Saral Jyotish 6	
	Saral Jyotish 7	
सरल षड्बल		

Contents

Chapter 1

Ayurveda and Astrology

There are many linkages between the ancient science of Ayurveda and Medical Astrology.

Both Astrology and Ayurveda diagnose a human's condition through the factors that surround them. Ayurveda takes the lens of nature and Astrology takes the lens of planets and stars.

A comparison between Ayurveda and Astrology is discussed to show the areas where these are of help.

The Ayurveda View

A very interesting story about the churning of the ocean of milk by Gods and Demons is given in the Bhagwat purana and Vishnu purana. Ocean of milk signifies the mind. It means that many valuable things emerge from introspection. In the same way, as the ocean was being churned, many valuable items emerged. The last to appear was the divine physician Danvantri.

Danvantri was holding a pot of nectar, which had the power of immortality. This signifies that immortality can be achieved only when the body and mind are in perfect state of health. And that a person who is mentally or physically sick cannot progress in life.

This nectar was distributed by Lord Vishnu who assumed the form of Mohini. Mohini stands for delusion of mind in the form of pride. As the story goes, the Demons were so enchanted by the form of Mohini that they forgot to partake of the nectar – they were full of pride and so they lost the battle of immortality.

Ayurveda is the traditional health care system of India which originated in the Vedic tradition. It provides a wealth of knowledge on how we can progress in life by keeping both our mind and body in good health.

Ayurvedic science is based on the fact that all matter, including humans, is composed of five basic elements - Earth, Water, Fire, Wind and Ether.

And each of these five elements has its own unique property:

Earth- Earth is the solid state of matter. It is stable. Parts of our body like bones, teeth, cells, flesh, body mass and tissues are manifestations of earth.

Water- It represents the liquid state of matter. It represents change, as water is not stable. A large part of our body is made of water. Water is used for two functions. One, is that our body stores water for future use. Two, body parts use water for their functioning. Fluids move between our cells to bring energy and eliminate waste. Water also controls our body temperature, fights disease and gives energy.

Fire- Fire has no substance but it can transform the state of any material. Fire is the energy which converts the food to fat. This energy controls our impulses, thought process and nervous system.

Air- Air is a gaseous form and is always moving and dynamic. Air helps fire to burn. Without air the life itself is not possible. Even all energy transfer is through air.

Ether- Ether fills the void between any two elements. It helps all elements to work and perform their functions. Without ether other elements cannot exist. Ether gives individuality to other elements. The function of ether is sound.

The Concept of Tridosha

The concept of Tridosha is unique to Ayurveda. Tridosha means a combination of three functional elements in our body. While the structural part of our body is made of five elements, but the functional aspect is governed by three humors or doshas.

These three doshas are Vata, Pitta and Kapha, and are always present in the body. They are present in every cell, tissue and organs. They govern all biological and pathological changes of the body. Each humor is a combination or Yoga of at least two elements.

As per Ayurveda, there are three doshas that are prevalent in our body: -

Vata- The elements of Vata are air and ether. It regulates movements and the nerve system. It controls all elimination of waste products.

Pitta-The elements of Pitta are fire and water. It causes all metabolism process in the body. It is from digestion of food and other transformation.

Kapha- The elements of Kapha are water and earth. It is the energy of cohesion and lubrication. It holds the body together.

Dosha or Yoga

In every human all three humors are always present in different proportions and form the constitution of a person. The basic constitution of a body is decided at the time of conception itself. It is called the **PRAKRUTI.** This should be maintained throughout life to stay healthy. When this basic constitution is disturbed, disease sets in and is called **VIKRUTI.**

In this way, when the three humors are in balance, the body is in **yoga state.** When the three humors are unbalanced, the body is in **dosha state.**

To understand a person, we must know his or her Prakruti. This helps in diagnosis of disease.

The Astrology View

Cause

Disease is caused by the vitiation of the three humors. Astrology believes that the motion of planets in the sky affect the human body. Each Nakshatra/planet represents a particular function of a part of body. When planets move in different Nakshatras they affect their respective body parts. Thus, both Ayurveda and astrology believe that the cause of disease is from an outside source and not within the body.

Diagnoses

In diagnosing a disease, the Ayurveda doctor measures the vitiation of a particular dosha and identifies the disease. Astrology does a similar analysis by reading the movements of planets. An Astrologer's diagnosis may not be as explicit as that of a doctor. But a good Astrologer can identify the occurrence of a disease even at the birth of a person.

Astrology can predict ahead of time, the disease which a person is likely to suffer in later life. By reading planetary movements, Astrology can foretell the occurrence of disease which is not possible for a physician.

Treatment

An Ayurveda doctor treats disease by prescribing medicines to balance the doshas. A doctor also focuses on the patient's symptoms. Many Ayurveda physicians refer to the astrological chart also. In a similar way, an astrologer reads planetary movements to predict what type of disease or the timing of disease may afflict a person. Not just that, each Nakshatra is linked to some herbs and plants, which may be consumed to address the disease. There are prayers and chants for each Nakshatra, which can also be practiced, to prevent or cure disease.

Each of the five basic elements that form our body - Earth, Water, Fire, Wind and Ether - are represented by the seven planets.

- Sun- Fire
- Moon- Water
- Mars- Fire
- Mercury- Earth
- Jupiter- Ether
- Venus- Water
- Saturn- Air

Brihat Parashar Hora Shastra identifies each planet with three humors.

- Sun; Bilious or Pitta
- Moon; Windy and phlegmatic or Vata and Kapha
- Mars; Bilious
- Mercury; all three
- Jupiter; Phlegmatic
- Venus; Windy and phlegmatic
- Saturn; Windy
- Rahu; Windy

If we know the planetary combinations for a person, we can read which of the three humors - Pitta, Vata, or Kapha are prevalent in a person.

Here are some examples. (This is not a comprehensive list.)

Vaat

1. Jupiter is placed in lagna and Saturn is in seventh house.

2. Mars is in seventh house or in trines with Saturn in lagna.

3.   Saturn and weak Moon in twelfth house gives serious disease.

4.   Saturn is debilitated and is related to sixth lord.

5.   Seventh lord is in lagna or seventh house.

Pitta

1.   Mercury and sixth lord are in trik house.

2.   Sun is in sixth house and is related with a malefic.

3.   Sun is in eighth house. Mars is weak and a malefic is in second house.

4.   Mars and lagna lord are in lagna or in eighth house without any benefic association or aspect.

5.   Lagna lord is in eighth house.

6.   Mercury is with sixth and eighth lord.

Kapha

1.   Sun and Saturn are conjunct.

2.   Sun or Moon is in fourth house and afflicted by Saturn.

3.   Mars occupies a malefic sign in Navamsha and is placed in sixth house with Mercury. Moon or Venus is related to them.

4.   Twelfth lord is in lagna.

Taste and cure

Ayurveda identifies six tastes. These are created by the combination or yoga of two basic elements. Each element is governed by a planet in astrology. This way each taste is linked with planets. These tastes will give rise to some humors and also diminish some. In a similar way planets also cause aggravation of some humors. These unbalanced humors are the cause of disease.

Thus, the affliction to the planets representing humors is the cause and indicates the onset of disease. The affliction to the constituent planets in birth charts is seen for promise of disorder in the body constitution. The affliction can also be seen during transit of malefic on the planets. When both factors show affliction, then it indicates the aggravation of disorders.

An Ayurveda doctor will use this knowledge to cure a disease. For example, a disorder caused by Kapha can be cured by giving medicine or food which decreases Kapha. Bitter taste decreases Kapha and thus can control the disorders of Kapha. We can link this to the transit of planets to indicate the time of relief. The transit of benefic or the bitter taste planets on the Kapha planets.

We will now discuss the tastes with its representation by planets, disease caused and the effect on humors.

Sweet:

Sweet taste is the yoga of earth and water. Earth is represented by Mercury and water is represented by Venus and Moon. It increases Kapha and decreases Vata and Pitta. The disorders caused are heaviness, cold, obesity, excess sleep, loss of appetite, diabetes, abnormal growth of muscles. The healing action is on skin and hair. It heals broken bones and promotes growth.

Sour:

It is the yoga of earth and fire. Earth is Mercury and fire is Sun and Mars. It increases Pitta and Kapha. It decreases Vata. The disorders caused are toxicity of blood, ulcer, sensitivity of teeth, heart burn, acidity, weakness and increased thirst. It stimulates appetite, sharpens mind and sense organs, good for heart and digestion.

Salty:

Salty taste is combination of water and fire. Water is Venus and Moon. Fire is Sun and Mars. It increases Pitta and Kapha and decreases Vata. The disorders are heating of body with fainting, weaken system, gout, and aggravate skin condition, gives wrinkles, hair fall, blood disorder, hypertension, peptic ulcer, rashes and pimples. It is helpful in digestion, retains water in body and nullifies the effect of other tastes.

Pungent:

Pungent is the yoga of fire and air. Fire is Sun and Mars. Air is Saturn. It increases Vata and Pitta. It decreases Kapha. Too much pungent can increase heat in body, causes weakness even unconsciousness and sweating. It improves taste of food and helps digestion by stimulating appetite. It improves circulation of blood, eliminates toxics, cleans body and removes blood clots. It cures disorders caused by Kapha.

Bitter:

It is combination of air and ether. The planet for air is Saturn and for ether is Jupiter. It increases Vata and decreases Pitta and Kapha. It can cause dehydration, increase roughness and reduces semen and bone marrow. It is most healing taste for imbalance of body and mind. It is anti-toxic and germicidal. It relives thirst, good for fever, promotes digestion and cleans blood.

Astringent:

It is mixture of air and earth. The planet for air is Saturn and for earth is Mercury. It increases Vata and decreases Pitta and Kapha. Excess astringent cause weakness and premature aging, constipation, and retention of gas. It promotes paralysis, spasm and has adverse effect on heart. It causes coagulation of blood. It helps to squeeze out excess water and reduces sweating and blood flow. It is anti-inflammatory and has sedative effect.

Chapter 2

Signs, Houses and Planets

In astrology, we have signs, houses and planets as the basic tools available to us. Each plays its role in indicating the problem area in medical astrology. We will underline their characteristics and the relation with the human body.

Signs

The twelve signs of the zodiac represent the parts of Kaal Purush. They also represent the five elements of nature.

The human body is divided in twelve parts and each part is represented by a sign.

Table of body parts by sign

Sign	External part	Internal part	Structural part
Aries	Head	Brain	Cerium bones
Taurus	Face	Larynx	Facial bones
Gemini	Neck, shoulders, arms, hand, upper chest	Wind pipe, upper food pipe	Bones of collar, neck, shoulder and arms
Cancer	Breast, Chest	Lungs, heart	Ribs
Leo	Upper abdomen	Upper spine, liver, spleen, duodomen, small intestine	Back bones, Upper spine

Sign	External part	Internal part	Structural part
Virgo	Lower abdomen	Bowles, large intestine	Lower spine
Libra	Region below naval, groins	Uterus, ovary, testicles, Kidney	Pelvic bones
Scorpio	Genital organs	Genitals, anus, lower part of large intestine	Lower back
Sagittarius	Thighs	Arteries	Hip bone
Capricorn	Knees	Joints	Kneecap joint
Aquarius	Legs, knuckle	Blood circulation	Shin bones
Pisces	Feet and toes	Lymphatic system	Bones of feet

The signs are also grouped as representative of elements.

Element	Signs	Represents
Fiery	Aries, Leo, Sagittarius	Vitality
Earthy	Taurus, Virgo, Capricorn	Flesh and bone
Airy	Gemini, Libra, Aquarius	Breathing
Watery	Cancer, Scorpio, Pisces	Blood

The Tridosha represented by signs are tabulated below.

Dosha	Signs
Vata	Gemini, Virgo, Libra, Capricorn, Aquarius
Pitta	Aries, Leo, Scorpio, Sagittarius
Kapha	Taurus, Cancer, Pisces

Planets

All nine planets are significators of various diseases and body parts. They also rule over the senses and humors of the body. The specific significations relevant to the matters of this presentation are given below for each planet.

Sun: Sun is bilious in nature. It is the giver of heat to the body. Life is sustained by the Sun. The Sun stands for energy, warmth and abundance.

Sun related diseases are high fever, burning in body, inflammation, headache and head disease, heart disease, palpitation, eye trouble specially, right eye, stomach, bones, epilepsy, skin disease, leucorrhea and leprosy.

Sun is significator of health. A good Sun gives freedom from disease. The strength of Sun is also checked in another related divisional chart.

Sun gives danger from wood, fire, poison, snakes and weapons.

The body parts governed by Sun are heart, bones, stomach, right eye and constitution of body.

Sun governs the sense of sight.

Moon: Moon is phlegmatic. It is the giver of ailments.

Diseases ruled by Moon are epilepsy, hidden ulcers in stomach, heart problems, consumption, TB, acidity, shoulder problems, ailments related to circulation of blood, anemia, cough cold, menstrual disorder, problems of breast and mammary glands, dysentery, typhoid, mental fatigue, mental problems like lunacy and sleep related problems.

Moon gives danger from water, horned animals, and watery creatures.

The body parts governed by Moon are heart, lungs, mind, blood, left eye, stomach, face, shoulders, and water in the body. (Most parts which thrive on water are governed by Moon. Venus governs the parts which treats water.)

Moon governs the sense of taste.

Mars: Mars is the significator of vitality and energy. It is bilious in nature and gives heat to body. Mars is stomach fire, governs bone marrow, Kidney, bladder, and pancreas.

The diseases given by Mars are wounds, disease of limbs, painful urination, coagulation of blood, leprosy, excessive thirst, eye problem, deformities, disease of upper part of body, high blood pressure, menstrual disorder, mental aggression, surgery, and abortion.

It gives danger from enemies, sons, brothers, king or person of authority and evil spirits.

The body parts ruled by Mars are blood (red corpuscles), bone marrow and appendix.

Mars also governs the sense of sight.

Mercury: Mercury is the mixture of all three doshas - windy, bilious, and phlegmatic. He governs brain, intelligence, and skin.

The diseases given are itching, skin disease, impotency, vertigo, and ENT disease.

It gives danger from food poisoning, fire, and problems due to hard labor.

Mercury controls the body moisture. It rules over skin, speech, neck, naval and sex organs, nose, spine, and throat. The higher body functions are also controlled by Mercury.

Mercury governs the sense of taste.

Jupiter: Jupiter is phlegmatic. It is the main significator of general physical health. He controls body strength, stamina, heart function, liver, ear, large intestine.

Diseases of Jupiter are jaundice, obesity, diabetic, ear disease, brain related problems like loss of memory or dysfunction of body parts due to brain ailment like paralysis.

It gives danger from Brahmins, due to disrespect to elders, preceptors, Gods and temples. It gives trouble due to hoarded wealth.

The body parts under Jupiter are digestive system, brain, knees, liver and attached parts like spleen, gall bladder and pancreas. Fat of body is governed by Jupiter.

Jupiter governs the sense of speech.

Venus: Venus is windy and phlegmatic. It is the luster of body. A good Venus gives well-proportioned body. He controls sugar levels, semen, and genital problems.

Diseases given by Venus are venereal diseases, weak eyesight, loss of body luster, cataract, nephritis, sexual incompetency, stone in kidney and urinary tract, leukoderma.

It gives fear from witches, female deities, and break in friendship.

It governs eyesight, semen, urinary system, genitals, and reproductive system.

Venus governs the sense of touch.

Saturn: Saturn is windy. He is the significator of ill health. He controls vitamins, calcium, legs and nerves.

It can cause lameness, stomach pains, bone fracture or damage to limbs, rheumatic pains, paralysis, insanity, cancer, depression, hysteria, deafness.

It gives danger from blow from wood or stone.

It governs legs, sense of touch in skin, joints and limbs, hair.

Rahu: Rahu is phlegmatic and windy. He controls worldly desires and material manifestation.

The diseases are lung trouble, difficult breathing, duodenal pains, phobias, ulcers and boils, epilepsy, poisoning, Hydrocele, hemorrhoids breathing, neck, legs and lungs.

It gives fear of burning, distress from child or spouse, from serpents and enemies.

Rahu controls breathing, feet and lower abdomen.

Ketu: It is the main cause of painful ulcers and tumors. Ketu is bilious in nature. He gives no interest in worldly desire due to spiritualism.

The diseases are caused by unknown source. It can give consumption, painful fever, wind complaint, diseases of stomach and eyes, ulcers, small pox, piles, surgery, infectious disease, worm or ulcers in intestine.

Ketu controls belly and feet.

It gives trouble through disputes with Brahmins and Kshatriya.

Gulika: Gulika causes problems due to poison (wrong medicine) and body pains.

Houses

House of a horoscope also signifies the body parts. The houses signify a wider range of body parts as compared to signs.

The right side of body is represented by the first to seventh house. The left side is represented by seventh to first house. In other words, the right side is represented by invisible half and left side by visible half of horoscope. Some scholars make a difference for male and female horoscope. The left side of female horoscope is represented by invisible half and right side by visible half. In another opinion the right side is seen from second to sixth house and left is seen from twelfth to eighth house in reverse order.

First house: Body in general (healthy or diseased), head, brain, mind, hair, skin, limbs, old age, strength, freedom from illness.

Second house: Face, nose, right eye, tongue, teeth, oral cavity, larynx, gullet, nails, bones and flesh.

Third house: Right ear, neck, shoulders, collar bones, clavicles, windpipe (trachea), breathing, food pipe (esophagus), first part of hand (between thumb and index finger), physical body growth, thyroid and mental status.

Fourth house: Heart, lungs, chest, diaphragm, and blood.

Fifth house; Heart (other opinion), upper abdomen, gall bladder, liver, pancreas, spleen, and small intestine.

Sixth house: Lower abdomen, large intestine, kidney, and appendix. It is house of disease.

Seventh house: Urinary tract, prostate gland, uterus, ovaries, testes, semen, and groins.

Eighth house: External genital, rectum, seminal vessels, and loss of limb.

Ninth house: Hips, thighs and anterior system (female).

Tenth house: Knee cap (patella), knee joint and popliteal fossa (hollow behind knee joint).

Eleventh house: Left ear, legs and shanks.

Twelfth house: Left eye, feet, crippled limbs and physical ailments.

Chapter 3

Nakshatra

There are 27 Nakshatra in Hindu astrology. Abhijit Nakshatra is also added between U. Ashadha and Shravan to make a total of 28 Nakshatra. Each Nakshatra has been assigned equal span of 13 degrees 20 minutes except Abhijit. At micro level this is not true. Each Nakshatra comprises of stars and the span of each Nakshatra cannot be same. These stars occupy different space in zodiac.

Siddhantashiromani written by Bhaskaracharya gives the micro span of each Nakshatra. It is recommended to use this span of Nakshatra for medical astrology. Table for micro longitudes of Nakshatra is given.

	Nakshatra	Starting Longitude Sign Deg. Min. Sec.
1	Ashwani	00 - 00 - 00 - 00
2	Bharani	00 - 13 - 10 - 35
3	Kritika	00 - 19 - 45 - 52
4	Rohini	01 - 02 - 56 - 27
5	Mrigshira	01 - 22 - 42 - 19
6	Ardra	02 - 05 - 52 - 54
7	Punarvasu	02 - 12 - 27 - 12
8	Pushya	03 - 02 - 14 - 04
9	Ashlesha	03 - 15 - 24 - 39
10	Magha	03 - 21 - 59 - 56
11	P. Phalguni	04 - 05 - 10 - 31
12	U. Phalguni	04 - 18 - 21 - 06
13	Hasta	05 - 08 - 06 - 58
14	Chitra	05 - 21 - 17 - 33

	Nakshatra	Starting Longitude Sign Deg. Min. Sec.
15	Swati	06 - 04 - 28 - 08
16	Visakha	06 - 11 - 03 - 26
17	Anuradha	07 - 00 - 49 - 18
18	Jyeshtha	07 - 13 - 59 - 53
19	Moola	07 - 20 - 35 - 10
20	P. Ashadha	08 - 03 - 45 - 45
21	U. Ashadha	08 - 16 - 56 - 20
22	Abhijit	09 - 06 - 42 - 12
23	Shravan	09 - 10 - 56 - 31
24	Dhanista	09 - 24 - 07 - 06
25	Shatbhisaj	10 - 07 - 17 - 41
26	P. Bhadrapad	10 - 13 - 52 - 58
27	U. Bhadrapad	10 - 27 - 03 - 33
28	Revati	11 - 16 - 49 - 25

The Nakshatra have been assigned a body portion and is of importance in locating the diseased part. The body parts are described in Purana. This is basically attributed as a worship tool. We assign the parts from head to toe in the order of Nakshatra. A table of body parts represented by Nakshatra is given.

Nakshatra and Body Parts

	Nakshatra	Body parts as per Purana	Body parts of Nakshatra
1	Ashwani	Both Knees	Head, cerebral hemisphere, top portion of feet, inner parts of head
2	Bharani	Head	Head, cerebral hemisphere, inner parts of eyes, bottom parts of feet

	Nakshatra	Body parts as per Purana	Body parts of Nakshatra
3	Kritika	Waist	Eyes, brain, vision, face, neck, lower jaw, hips, loins, crown of head, throat
4	Rohini	Both legs	Forehead, face, ankles, shin, calves of legs, mouth, tongue, tonsils, palate, neck, cerebellum, cervical
5	Mrigshira	Two eyes	Face, chin, cheeks, larynx, palate, throat, vocal cord, arms, shoulders, thymus gland, upper ribs, eye and eye brows
6	Ardra	Hair	Throat, arms, shoulders, chest, back and front of head, brain controlling mechanism, nervous system
7	Punarvasu	Fingers	Ear, nose, throat, shoulder blades, lungs, respiratory system, chest, stomach, esophagus, diaphragm, pancreas, upper lobe of liver
8	Pushya	Mouth	Lungs, stomach, ribs, face
9	Ashlesha	Nails	Lungs, stomach, esophagus, diaphragm, pancreas, liver, bone joints like elbow, knuckle, knee cap, ears
10	Magha	Nose	Heart, back, spinal cord, spleen, dorsal region of spine, aorta, lips, chin
11	P. Phalguni	Private parts	Heart, spinal cord, sex organs, lips, right hand
12	U. Phalguni	Private parts	Abdomen, liver function, lips, sex organs, left hand

	Nakshatra	Body parts as per Purana	Body parts of Nakshatra
13	Hasta	Two hands	Intestine, liver, spine
14	Chitra	Forehead	Belly, lower part, kidney, loins, hernia, vasomotor system, neck, lower part of spine
15	Swati	Teeth	Skin, kidney, urethra, appendicitis, hernia, bladder, chest, parts through which air circulates in body
16	Visakha	Both upper limbs	Lower abdomen, parts near bladder, pancreatic glands, genitals, rectum, descending colon, prostrate, arms and breasts
17	Anuradha	Heart	Bladder, genital organs, rectum, nasal bones near genital organs, breast, womb, bowels
18	Jyeshtha	Tongue	Colon, anus, genitals, ovaries, womb, neck, right side of torso
19	Moola	Both feet	Hips, thighs, femur, ileum, sciatica nerve, right side of torso
20	P. Ashadha	Thighs	Hips, coccygeal and sacral region of spine, filial arteries and veins, back (neck to waist)
21	U. Ashadha	Thighs	Femur, arteries, skin, knees, waist

	Nakshatra	Body parts as per Purana	Body parts of Nakshatra
22	Shravan	Two ears	Lymphatic vessels, knees, skin, brain action, sex organs
23	Dhanista	Back	Knee cap, ankles, limbs, portion between knee and ankles, anus, spinal chord
24	Shatbhisaj	Both side of chin	Knees and ankles, calf muscle, jaws, act of eating, speaking, right thigh
25	P Bhadrapad	Side of body	Left side of body, ankle, feet, toe, ribs, sides of leg, left thigh, sole of feet, side of abdomen
26	U Bhadrapad	Side of body	Feet, right side of body, right side of legs, abdomen, sole of feet
27	Revati	Both armpits	Feet and toes, ankles, groin

Nakshatra and Disease

	Nakshatra	Diseases
1	Ashwani	Headache, mental illness, smallpox, malaria, head injury, insomnia, brain affliction, accident, epilepsy, paralyses, meningitis, cerebral hemorrhage, loss of memory
2	Bharani	Venereal disease, face, head injury, cataract and eye disease, giddiness, knee pain, arthritis, high fever, laziness
3	Kritika	Tonsils, headache, fevers, inflammation, smallpox, eyesight, burns and scalds, accident by explosives, filarial, tonsillitis, nasal polypus

	Nakshatra	**Diseases**
4	Rohini	Cold and cough, irregular menses, apoplexy, obesity, venereal disease, stress related problems, problem in ribs and lungs, pneumonia
5	Mrigshira	Sciatica, sore throat, shoulder pain, disease due to excessive water consumption, mumps, ear problem, shoulders, urinary problem, difficult breathing
6	Ardra	Nervous system disorder, allergies, lungs problems, asthma, mental disorders, skin sensitivity, paralysis
7	Punarvasu	ENT, diabetic, asthma, TB, jaundice, pneumonia, bronchitis, lumbago, pleurisy, otitis, goiter, pulmonary tuberculosis, goiter, bronchitis
8	Pushya	Eczema, ulcers, nausea, breast cancer, TB, gastric problems, cancer, gall stone, water retention, jaundice, liver, xanthopsia, fits
9	Ashlesha	Poor diet, obesity, venereal disease, arthritis, nephritis, oedema, jaundice, breathing problem
10	Magha	Skin problem around mouth, heart, stomach disorders, unconsciousness, spine, palpitation, mental disease
11	P. Phalguni	Addictions, heart, blood circulation, dental problems, myocarditis, high BP, nerve, spine, pain in toes, anemic
12	U. Phalguni	Digestive trouble, hands and arms, skin, dental problems, headache, liver, constipation, back ache, high BP

	Nakshatra	**Diseases**
13	Hasta	Bowles, dysentery, colon, cold and allergies, disease due to water, high blood pressure, cholera, artery and veins, hysteria
14	Chitra	Ulcers, sun stroke, insect bites, kidney, excess urine, brain fever, stomach ulcers, intestine worms
15	Swati	Urinary problems, intestinal problems, eczema, brights disease, skin, appendicitis,
16	Visakha	Prostrate, piles, colon problems, diabetes, paralysis, testes, uterus
17	Anuradha	Constipation, piles, irregular menses, womb problems, breast, cough and cold
18	Jyeshtha	Neck pain, wind, gout, fertility problems, fistula, pain in arms, anus, white discharge, aids,
19	Moola	Mental problems, obesity, foot problems, joint pains, hips, low BP, breathing problem
20	P. Ashadha	Bladder, kidney problems, rheumatism, lungs, diabetes, blood poisoning, cold, water retention
21	U. Ashadha	Stomach problems, eczema, arthritis, skin dryness, breathing difficult, paralysis, weak digestion, palpitation, eye
22	Shravan	Hearing problems, reproductive organ disease, sensitive skin, urinary problems, lameness, knees, weak digestion
23	Dhanista	Arthritis, back problems, hypertension, piles, heart problems, ankles, broken limbs, high BP
24	Shatbhisaj	Jaw problems, fracture of bones, high blood pressure, rheumatism, heart disease, problems due to water

	Nakshatra	Diseases
25	P. Bhadrapad	Swelling of feet, heart problems, enlarged liver, ulcers, low BP, jaundice, hernia
26	U. Bhadrapad	Cold feet, indigestion, stress disorders, allergies, liver problems, intestine, TB
27	Revati	Childhood illness, insomnia, sensitive nervous system, pain in feet, ulcer in intestine, deafness

Deities of Nakshatra

	Nakshatra	Deity	Description
1	Ashwani	Ashwani Kumar	Twins. Physicians of Gods. A physician cures the disease given by the planet. Moves in a three-wheeled chariot to cure the Gods. Some scholars take Ganesh as deity of Ashwani star. **Can give two diseases**.
2	Bharani	Yama	God of death. He lays down the right conduct. Planet afflicted gives aggravation due to bad conduct and **lack of self-discipline**.
3	Kritika	Agni	Fire God. Full of energy and activity. When afflicted then the **energy is lost**.
4	Rohini	Brahma	Celestial father. Afflicted planets can give **genetic problems**. Well placed provide father like protection.

5	Mrigshira	Moon	Medicines. Freedom from illness. It desires to search worldly pleasures like a deer that keeps on roaming. Affliction causes multiple illnesses. Disease due to egoistic nature. **The strength is movement.**
6	Ardra	Rudra	Rudra means sufferings and fear. As Shiva he is great healer. It therefore denotes change from suffering to healing. Afflicted planet can give serious problems. Rudra is leader of **nervous system.**
7	Punarvasu	Aditi	Mother of Sun God. This star gives Lot of activity. Power to **regain vitality** is present. It gives repetition of health and illness.
8	Pushya	Brihaspati	Guru of Gods. **Good counseling** gives protection from disease.
9	Ashlesha	Serpents	Snakes reside underground or in water. Planets in this position can cause **water borne disease**. The disease **deep inside** the body is also caused. When well connected, it gives freedom from poison. Sight of a serpent.

10	Magha	Pitra	Departed elders. It denotes the earlier generations. The **ancestor's** hands down the ailment or good health.
11	P. Phalguni	Bhaga	Enjoyment. Likes to look beautiful and undergoes treatment for this. Self centered and takes care of body. Cannot tolerate **ugliness** of disease.
12	U. Phalguni	Aryaman	Helpful. Planets in this portion provide help in keeping the strength of body. It shows the **way to cure the body.**
13	Hasta	Aditya	First ray of Sun. It is end of night and start of day. Getting rid of the ailments and starting a new day. This star has **curative power**.
14	Chitra	Twashta	The architect. Creates with five elements. Care free from end results. The good or bad health is his **own creation**.
15	Swati	Vayu	Life breath. Air is wandering everywhere and indicates **unsteady body and mind**. The health of body and mind is not stable.

16	Visakha	Indragni	Indra and Agni. Indra was disgraced for forbidden act. Such planet ruins health by **overindulgence**. Agni is fire and can destroy anything.
17	Anuradha	Mitra	Friend. Cannot live without friends. This is the root cause of cure as well as illness. **Uncontrolled liking** can be harmful and ruin body and mind.
18	Jyeshtha	Indra	In this position, an afflicted planet **acts badly** and cause harm to body. When not afflicted gives a sound health.
19	Moola	Nirriti	Goddess of death. The worldly attachments are destroyed and progress toward spiritual is granted. The person is **careless about his body** problems and do not want to be cured.
20	P. Ashadha	Jala	Water. Deep inside. **Water related problems** or cure by water.
21	U. Ashadha	Vishvadev	God of universe. Protector and provider to whole body. It stands for **general strength**. When afflicted can give weak body.

22	Shravan	Vishnu	Preserver. Takes care of the needs of body and nourishes it. Normally gives **good health**. When afflicted the recovery is difficult.
23	Dhanista	Ashtavasu	Vasus give protection and **good health**. When afflicted it punish the afflicting planet.
24	Shatbhisaj	Varun	Lord of water. He is the giver of nectar of life. He holds a pitcher and cures all ailments. When afflicted it can give **disease of water**.
25	P. Bhadrapad	Ajakapat	One footed goat. Lord Shiva performed Tandav by balancing his body on one foot. It gives **destruction** of disease or the body itself.
26	U. Bhadrapad	Ahir Budhnya	Serpent of island. Lower part is of a snake and upper part is like God. Lower part is protected by upper part. It is **protective and destructive** at the same time.
27	Revati	Opusan	Prosperous. He is lord of light and dispeller of darkness. Planet shows new light and **cure by change of treatment**.

Nakshatra, Tridosha and Duration of Disease

When a disease starts in a particular Nakshatra, then the duration of illness is given.

	Nakshatra	**Dosha**	**Duration**
1	Ashwani	Vata Airy	1, 9, 25 days
2	Bharani	Pitta Fiery	11, 21, 30 days. Can be fatal
3	Kritika	Kapha Watery	9/10, 21 days
4	Rohini	Kapha	3/7/9 or 10 days
5	Mrigshira	Pitta	3, 5, 9 days
6	Ardra	Vata	10, 30 days. Can be fatal.
7	Punarvasu	Vata	7, 9 days
8	Pushya	Pitta	7 days
9	Ashlesha	Kapha	9, 20, 30 days. Generally it is fatal.
10	Magha	Kapha	20, 30, 45 days. Disease can repeat.
11	P. Phalguni	Pitta	8, 15, 30 days. Can last for one year.
12	U. Phalguni	Vata	7, 15, 27 days.
13	Hasta	Vata	7, 8, 9, 15 days. Sometimes disease can repeat.
14	Chitra	Pitta	8, 11, 15 days. Can be fatal.
15	Swati	Kapha	1, 2, 5, 10 months. Can give complicated disease.
16	Visakha	Kapha	8, 10, 20, 30 days.
17	Anuradha	Pitta	6, 10, 28 days.
18	Jyeshtha	Vata	15, 21 30 days. Can be fatal.
19	Moola	Vata	9, 15, 20 days.
20	P. Ashadha	Pitta	15 to 20 days. Can go for 2, 3, 6 months.
21	U. Ashadha	Kapha	20, 45 days.
22	Shravan	Kapha	3, 6, 10, 25 days.

	Nakshatra	Dosha	Duration
23	Dhanista	Pitta	13, 15 days.
24	Shatbhisaj	Vata	3, 10, 21, 40 days.
25	P. Bhadrapad	Vata	2, 10 days. Can be for 2 to 3 months.
26	U. Bhadrapad	Pitta	7, 10, 45 days.
27	Revati	Kapha	10, 28, 45 days.

Nakshatra, plants and Curative Use

Nakshatra	Plant name	Botanical name	Part used	Curative use
Ashwani	1. Kutaki	1. Picronhizea	1. Root	1. Meningitis, high fever
	2. Rakhi Phool	2. Passiflora quadrangles	2. Leaves	2. Spasm
	3. Coffee	3. Coffee arabica	3. Seeds, leaves	3. Migraine
Bharani	1. Eranda oil 2. Dhataki 3. Gwar Patha 4. Isabgole	1. Ricinus communis 2. Woodfordia fruiicosa 3. Aloe vera 4. Plantago major	1. Root, leaves, seed oil 2. Flower 3. Flower, leaves 4. Full plant	1. Liver disorder 2. Vaginal discharge 3. Pulmonary catarrh 4. Mucus reins
Kritika	1. Harsingar 2. Chawal	1. Nyctanthus arbortristis 2. Oryza sativa	1. Leaves, bark 2. Seeds, leaves	1. Malaria 2. Piles, indigestion
Rohini	1. Kantakari	1. Solanum xanthocer-pum	1. Leaf, ower, fruit, seed, bark, stem	Cough, bronchial asthama
Mrigshira	1. Shunti 2. Onion 3. Kuchla	1. Zingiber offtinale 2. Allium cepa 3. Strychnos nuxvomica	1. Stem 2. Bulb, leaves 3. Seeds, fruit	1. Indigestion, atulence 2. Pain, sciatica, fever, skin 3. Itching, haemoptyasis

Nakshatra	Plant name	Botanical name	Part used	Curative use
Ardra	1. Pipata 2. Tambakoo	1. Ficus mligiosa 2. Nicotiana tabacum	1. Bark, fruit, leaf 2. Leaves	1. Bronchial asthma, bronchitis 2. Eosinophila, giddiness, injury
Punarvasu	1. Hing 2. Kalmegh 3. Arka	1. Ferula foetida 2. Andrographis paniculata 3. Calatropis	1. Latex 2. Root, stem, fruit, leaves 3. Root, lower, leaves	1. Indigestion, gastritis 2. Liver disorder 3. Dropsy, worms
Pushya	1. Babool 2. Kutaja 3. Vijaysar 4. Hadjod	1. Aicacia arebica 2. Holarrhena anilidysentehca 3. Ptemcaipus santotinus 4. Vitis quadrangularis	1. Bark, leaf, stem, gum, fruit 2. Seed, bark 3. Bark 4. Stem, leaves	1. Dental disorder, pyorrhea 2. Diarrhoea, dysentery 3. Diabetes 4. Diarrhoea, bone
Ashlesha	1. Sonpha 2. Tulsi 3. Kasni	1. Foeniculum vugare 2. Ocimum sanctum 3. Cichorium endivia	1. Seeds, fruit 2. Seed, leaf 3. Root	1. Diarrhoea, dysentery, indigestion 2. Cough 3. Dyspepsia
Magha	1. Shirisha 2. Rasna	1. Albizzia lebbeck 2. Vanda roxburgxii	1. Bark, seed, leaf, lower 2. Seed	1. Bronchial asthma 2. Arthritis, gout
P. Phalguni	1. Pudina 2. Satavari 3. Apple	1. Mentha virktis 2. Asparagus officinalis 3. Pyrus malus	1. Stem, leaf 2. Stem 3. Fruit	1. Vomiting 2. Tonic 3. Cardiac problem, aneursm

Nakshatra	Plant name	Botanical name	Part used	Curative use
U. Phalguni	1. Bel 2. Neem	1. Aegle mamelos 2. Azadirachta indica	1. Bark, root, leaf, fruit 2. Leaves, lowers, bark, fruit	1. Diarrhoea, dysentery, heart disease 2. Piles, scabies, bowels disorder
Hasta	1. Palasha 2. Dhania 3. Lunuk	1. Butea monosperrma 2. Coriandrium sativum 3. Portulaca oleracea	1. Seed, leaf, bark, fower 2. Seed, root, fower, stem 3. Fruit, leaf	1. Worm infection 2. Typhoid, fever 3. Anxiety, fever
Chitra	1. Vidanga 2. Ashoka 3. Ashwag-andha 4. Kapik-achhu 5. Beltari	1. Emblia ribes 2. Saraca indica 3. Withania somnifera 4. Mucuna prunius 5. Bryonia alba	1. Fruit 2. Bark, seed, fower 3. Root 4. Root, seed 5. Fruit, leaves	1. Worm infection 2. Heart tonic 3. Hypertension, neurosis 4. Neurosis worms 5. Fever
Swati	1. Kanta karanja	1. Caesalpinia bonducella	1. Root, seed, fruit	1. Malaria, eczema
Visakha	1. Bharangi 2. Haridra	1. Cterodendron senatum 2. Curcuma longa	1. Root 2. Stem	1. Bronchial asthama 2. Diabetes, wounds, asthama, uraemina
Anuradha	1. Parasika yavani 2. Afim	1. Hyoscyamus niger 2. Papavar somnifervum	1. Leaf, seed 2. Latex, seed	1. Pain in abdomen, cough, diarrhea 2. Narcotic effects

Nakshatra	Plant name	Botanical name	Part used	Curative use
Jyeshtha	1. Vidhara 2. Anvia 3. Haritiki 4. Lodra	1. Lettsoinia nervosa 2. Emblica offidnalis 3. Terminalia chebula 4. Symplocus recemosa	1. Leaves 2. Fruit 3. Fruit 4. Root, leaves, fruit, bud	1. Cuteneous affections 2. Peptic ulcer, uterine ulcer 3. Constipation, piles, bowels, fistula 4. Vaginal discharge, leucorrhoea
Moola	1. Bhringraj	1. Eclipta alba	1. Leaves	1. Peptic ulcer
P. Ashadha	1. Bargad	1. Ficus bangalensia	1. Bark, leaves, fruit, stem	1. Diabetes
U. Ashadha	1. Bakuchi	1. Psoralia corylifolia	1. Seed oil, seeds	1. Leucoderma
Shravan	1. Punamava 2. Apamarg 3. Bishlo-omba 4. Adusa	1. Boerhaavia drffusa 2. Acbyranthes aspera 3. Citrullus cotosynthis 4. Adhatoda vasica	1. Root seed, leaf, lower, fruit, stem 2. Root, seed, leaf, lower, fruit, stem 3. Root, leaves 4. Root, leaf, lower	1. Oedema 2. Leprosy 3. Gout, rheumatism 4. Cough
Dhanista	1. Lashaun	1. Allium sativum	1. Stem, oil	1. Indigestion, heart tonic
Shatbhisaj				
P. Bhadrapad	1. Sankha-pushpi	1. Evotwkis	1. Root, stem, fruit	1. Anxiety, neurosis, mild hypertension

Nakshatra	Plant name	Botanical name	Part used	Curative use
U. Bhadrapad	1. Gokharu 2. Guggul 3. Karpoor	1. Tribulus tenesths 2. Commiphom mukul 3. Cinnamonium camphora	1. Root, seed, leaf, lower, fruit, stem 2. Latex 3. Latex, root	1. Urinary tract, infection, fever 2. Arthritis 3. Sprain, anodyne
Revati	1. Baheda 2. Guduchi 3. Chirboli 4. Badi saunf	1. Terminalia berica 2. Tinospora cardifolia 3. Physalis indica 4. Pimpinella anethum	1. Bark 2. Stem 3. Leaves, bark 4. Roots, fruit	1. Heart tonic 2. Fever 3. Gout 4. Flatulence, abdominal

Chapter 4

Divisional Charts

Divisional charts play an important role in diagnosis, location and timing of disease. The timing of occurrence and cure of disease can be seen from these charts. Beside the birth chart and Navamsha we use the following five divisional charts. Each of these charts has a specific use in medical astrology. These charts are-

1.   Drekkana

2.   Shashtamsha

3.   Shodashamsha

4.   Saptvimshamsha

5.   Trimshamsha

Drekkana

Each sign is divided in three equal parts of 10 degrees each. Planet in first Drekkana (0 – 10 degree) remains in the same sign as occupied by it in D1.

Planet in second Drekkana (10 – 20 degree) goes to fifth sign from the sign occupied by it in D1.

Planet in third Drekkana (20 – 30 degree) moves to ninth sign from the sign occupied by it in D1.

A table for working Drekkana chart is given.

Parashar Drekkana											
Sign	**Ari**	**Tau**	**Gem**	**Can**	**Leo**	**Vir**	**Lib**	**Sco**	**Sag**	**Cap**	**Aqu**	**Pis**
00 – 10°	Ari	Tau	Gem	Can	Leo	Vir	Lib	Sco	Sag	Cap	Aqu	Pis
10° – 20°	Leo	Vir	Lib	Sco	Sag	Cap	Aqu	Pis	Ari	Tau	Gem	Can
20° – 30°	Sag	Cap	Aqu	Pis	Ari	Tau	Gem	Can	Leo	Vir	Lib	Sco

The three Drekkana of each sign represent the body parts. These are indicated by the Drekkana occupied by a planet and the house in the Drekkana chart.

The human body is divided into three parts. These are:

1.   First part is from head to neck.

2.   Second part is from neck to naval

3.   Third part is from naval to feet

The rising Drekkana is the first part. For example, if the lagna is 23 degrees then the Drekkana from 20 to 30 degrees is the rising or the first part. The second part will be from 0 to 10 degrees and third part will be from 10 to 20 degrees. Planets in the respective part will represent the body parts by its occupation of house in Drekkana chart as given in the table below. **In another opinion it is the sign occupied in Drekkana. This gives better results. We are taking this version.**

Body Parts as Per Drekkana			
House/ sign	**Rising Drekkana**	**Second Drekkana**	**Third Drekkana**
1	Head	Neck	Abdomen
2	Right eye	Right shoulder	Right generative organ and anus
3	Right ear	Right arm	Right testicle
4	Right nostril	Right Side of body	Right thigh
5	Right cheek	Right breast	Right knee
6	Right jaw	Right belly	Right shank
7	Mouth	Naval	Legs and Feet
8	Left Jaw	Left belly	Left shank

Body Parts as Per Drekkana			
House/ sign	Rising Drekkana	Second Drekkana	Third Drekkana
9	Left cheek	Left breast	Left knee
10	Left nostril	Left Side of body	Left thigh
11	Left ear	Left arm	Left testicle
12	Left eye	Left shoulder	Left generative organ and anus

These parts are given in reference to marks or scars on these parts on the body of new born baby. A malefic in a part or aspects it then it produces scars due to hurt or wounds. If benefic is in the part or aspects it then it gives moles, black mark, clot of hair or til. If the planets are in own sign, own Navamsha or in the Navamsha of fixed sign then marks are natural and seen from birth, otherwise these are produced subsequently. This helps us to decide the timing of onset of problems.

Internal and external

A good use of Drekkana is in deciding the indication of area of problem. The problem can be in an internal area of the part or it can be in an external area. Each Drekkana is further divided in two equal parts of 5 degrees each. The first five degrees of each Drekkana (0 to 5, 10 to 15 and 20 to 25 degrees) of a planet in any sign indicate internal area of the part. The last five degrees of each Drekkana (5 to 10, 15 to 20 and 25 to 30 degrees) of a planet in any sign indicate external area of the part. For example, Sun is at 16 degrees in Aries and is in second Drekkana. Thus, Sun indicates the internal part and governs the right side of heart. The sign occupied by Sun in Drekkana chart is Leo. Our observation is a result of examination of practical charts.

Example DOB 13 April 1939 TOB 04.00 POB Delhi

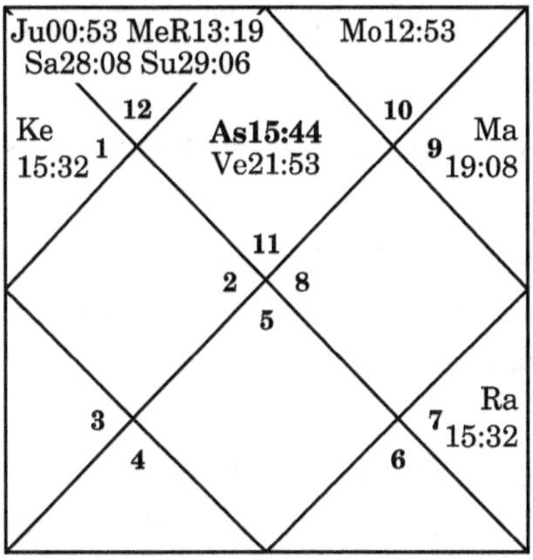

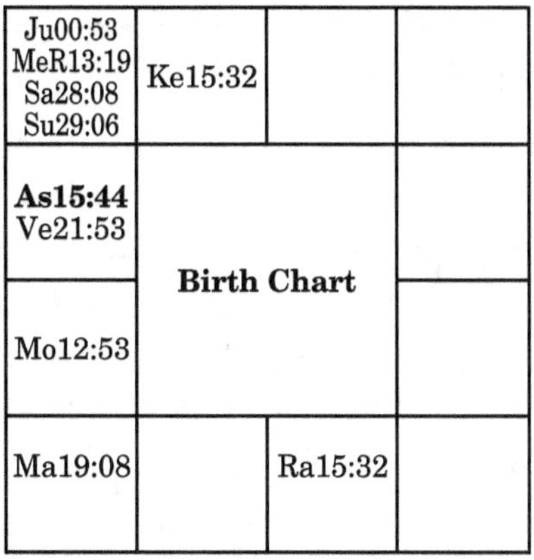

The rising or first Drekkana is 10 to 20 degrees and represents from head to neck. The next Drekkana 20 to 30 degrees represent neck to naval and Drekkana from 0 to 10 degrees represent naval to feet. Planets in respective Drekkana indicate body parts in accordance to the Drekkana part and the sign occupied in Drekkana. Please note that the sign occupied is important and not house.

The part of body and the area represented by each planet is tabulated for easy understanding.

	Planet	Drek-kana	Sign in D3	Part of D3	Body part	Area
1	Sun	Second	Scorpio	Second	Left belly	External
2	Moon	Rising	Taurus	First	Right eye	Internal
3	Mars	Rising	Aries	Second	Head	External
4	Mercury	Rising	Cancer	First	Right nostril	Internal
5	Jupiter	Third	Pisces	Third	anus	Internal
6	Venus	Second	Libra	First	Naval	Internal
7	Saturn	Second	Scorpio	Second	Left belly	External
8	Rahu	Rising	Aquarius	Second	Left ear	External
9	Ketu	Rising	Leo	Second	Right cheek	External

Six planets indicate internal parts of body. The diseases caused by them are in the internal organs.

Shashtamsha

This divisional chart is given in Jaimini sutra. It is referred as Kaulaka.

Each sign is divided into six equal parts. Each part measures five degrees (5^0).

For planets in odd signs, the first Shashtamsha occupies Aries. For planets in even signs, the first Shashtamsha occupies Libra. The next part moves in the direct order. This method of casting is cyclical.

This chart is seen for proneness to physical illness and its cure. The general health is studied. The Saptvimshamsha chart shows the general strength of the body and the resistance to disease. This chart shows the onset of disease.

A table for casting Shashtamsha chart is given.

Cyclical Shashtamsha – D6			
Part	Degrees	Odd Signs	Even Signs
1	5°	Ari	Lib
2	10°	Tau	Sco
3	15°	Gem	Sag
4	20°	Can	Cap
5	25°	Leo	Aqu
6	30°	Vir	Pis

House Signification

Lagna – General proneness to disease. Self-acquired problems.

Second House – Eating habits and the effect there from on the health. A benefic is welcome here.

Third House – Capacity to fight disease. Benefic aspect is required to ensure health and freedom from enemy or disease.

Fourth House – Support of family in maintaining health. The planet associated with fourth house is the support giver.

Fifth House – Problems or comfort due to Poorva Punya. The mental attitude towards illness. Diseases which are present at the time of birth.

Sixth House – Curable disease. Outward illness.

Seventh House – Helping hands or troublemakers.

Eighth House – Chronic or incurable disease.

Ninth House – Luck factor in dealing with diseases.

Tenth House – Problems created by own action or inaction.

Eleventh House – Sixth from sixth house and the strongest Upchaya house. Expansion of disease and problems.

Twelfth House – confinement, release from disease.

Jaimini gives the cause of disease by the placement of afflicting planet in different Kaulaka. These are reproduced below.

If the afflicting planet is in the first Kaulaka, the disease/injury will be in the forehead (3.3.60).

If the afflicting planet is in the second Kaulaka, there will be disease in the hair (3.3.61).

If the afflicting planet is in the third Kaulaka, blood disorder/disease will result (3.3.62).

If the afflicting planet is in the fourth Kaulaka, eye diseases will result (3.3.63).

If the afflicting planet is in the 5th Kaulaka, danger from wild cats and lions exists (3.3.64).

If the afflicting planet is in the 6th Kaulaka, diseases of the tongue (mouth/throat) could result (3.3.64).

Shashtamsha chart for the example horoscope is given.

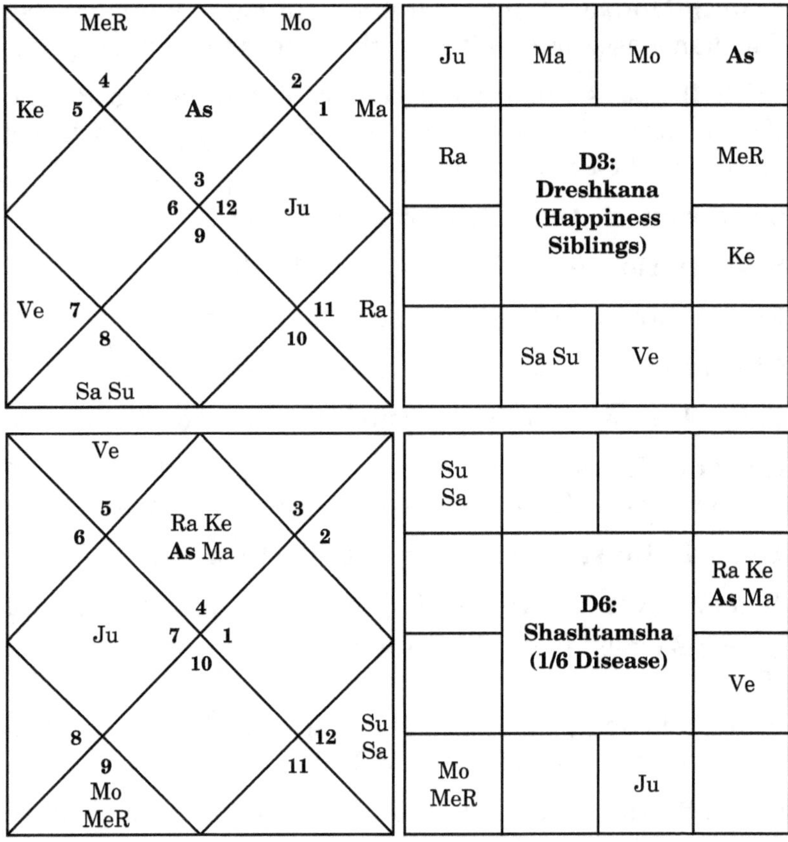

Lagna has three Malefic and is a disease prone chart. Lagna lord is in 6th house and is aspected by 8th lord Saturn. Mercury is also in 6th house. The disease was at peak in Mercury dasha. Saturn is the afflicting planet. It is in 6th Kaulaka and the disease is from mouth or tongue. It is not so. He suffered from stomach ailments which can be related to mouth indirectly.

Shodashamsha

Shodashamsha is one sixteenth division of a sign. It is also known as Kalamsha or Niripmanamsha.

Each sign is divided into sixteen equal parts resulting 1^0–52'–30" as the span of one part and is the measure of one Shodashamsha.

The first Shodashamsha of planets placed on movable sign remains in Aries. The next Shodashamsha goes to next sign in direct order to Taurus and so on.

For planets placed in fixed sign, the first Shodashamsha goes to Leo and the rest follows in direct order.

For planets placed in dual sign the first Shodashamsha goes to Sagittarius and the rest follows in direct order.

A table for casting of Shodashamsha is given.

Table for casting D16			
Part	Degrees	(Movable) Ari, Can, Lib, Cap	(Fixed) Tau, Leo, Sco, Aqu	(Dual) Gem, Vir, Sag, Pis
1	01°–52'–30"	Ari	Leo	Sag
2	03°–45'–00"	Tau	Vir	Cap
3	05°–37'–30"	Gem	Lib	Aqu
4	07°–30'–00"	Can	Sco	Pis
5	09°–22'–30"	Leo	Sag	Ari
6	11°–15'–00"	Vir	Cap	Tau
7	13°–07'–30"	Lib	Aqu	Gem
8	15°–00'–00"	Sco	Pis	Can
9	16°–52'–30"	Sag	Ari	Leo
10	18°–45'–00"	Cap	Tau	Vir
11	20°–37'–30"	Aqu	Gem	Lib
12	22°–30'–00"	Pis	Can	Sco
13	24°–22'–30"	Ari	Leo	Sag
14	26°–15'–00"	Tau	Vir	Cap
15	28°–07'–30"	Gem	Lib	Aqu
16	30°–00'–00"	Can	Sco	Pis

As mentioned in the Brihat Parashar Hora Shastra

शोडषांष के सुखाऽसुखस्य विज्ञानं वाहनानां च।

From Shodashamsha one should assess the happiness and vehicles. Shodashamsha is the indicator of movable pleasures or happiness. The movable pleasures may be derived from materialistic things, sensual and mental satisfaction. Basically, this amount to the experience of happiness. We can say that this chart is the indicator of the nectar of life (रास). This chart is therefore seen for happiness or unhappiness during a dasha period. This is helpful in deciding the timing of cure or to undertake major medical decisions like surgery etc.

This chart is also called Kalamsha i.e. sixteen phases of Moon. Moon phases are from total darkness (Amavasya) to full brightness (Poornima). Moon is the indicator of mind (मन). This chart therefore is seen for "how much a person is able to enjoy the happiness available to him."

Moon also governs the mental strength and the patience of a person. The mental endurance is thus seen from Shodashamsha. On the negative side it is the mirage of pleasures which may lead to humiliation and unhappiness.

Planets associated with benefic or lord of benefic house and placed in angles/ trine are giver of happiness. For physical happiness Sun is the significator and should not be afflicted. Jupiter is the significator of general well-being.

Shodashamsha chart of example horoscope is given.

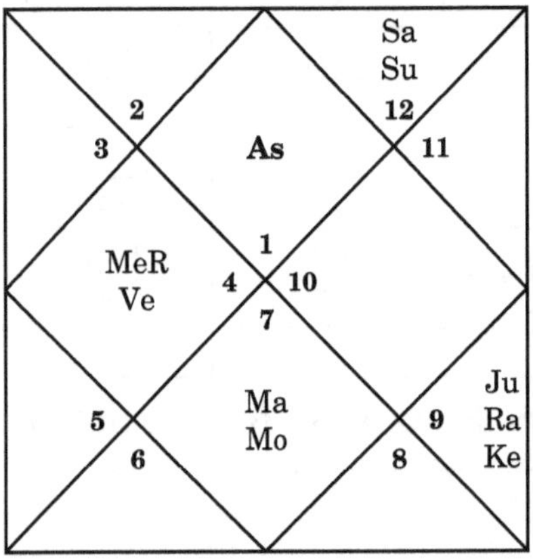

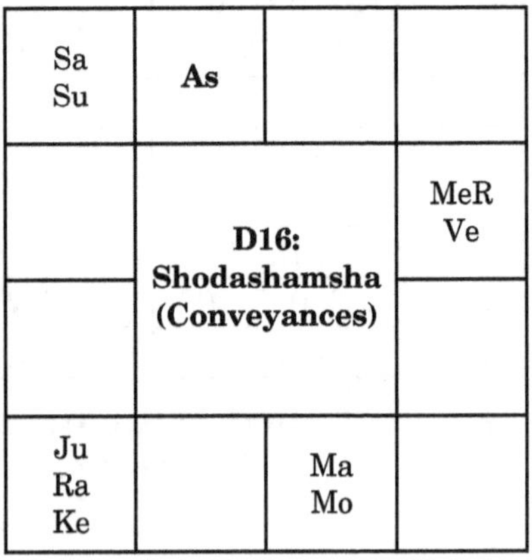

In this chart Sun and Jupiter are with Saturn or aspected by Saturn. Mercury is 3rd and 6th lord placed in fourth house. Benefic in fourth is good but with its bad lordship it gives problem in its dasha.

Saptvimshamsha

This is the most important chart for diagnosis of disease.

Each sign is divided into 27 equal parts. Each division of Saptvimshamsha is 1 deg 6 min 40 sec (1^0 6'40").

The first Saptvimshamsha of a planet in fiery signs (Aries, Leo, Sagittarius) start from Aries, of earthy signs (Taurus, Virgo, Capricorn) starts from Cancer, of Airy signs (Gemini, Libra, Aquarius) starts from Libra and of watery sign (Cancer, Scorpio, Pisces) starts from Capricorn. The other Saptvimshamsha occupy the next signs onward in direct order. The casting is cyclical.

Saptvimshamsha table for casting is given.

Saptvimshamsha (D27) Divisions					
Part	Degrees	Fiery (1,5,9)	Earthy (2,6,10)	Airy (3,7,11)	Watery (4,8,12)
1	01°–06'–40"	Ari	Can	Lib	Cap
2	02°–13'–20"	Tau	Leo	Sco	Aqu
3	03°–20'–00"	Gem	Vir	Sag	Pis
4	04°–26'–40"	Can	Lib	Cap	Ari
5	05°–33'–20"	Leo	Sco	Aqu	Tau
6	06°–40'–00"	Vir	Sag	Pis	Gem
7	07°–46'–40"	Lib	Cap	Ari	Can
8	08°–53'–20"	Sco	Aqu	Tau	Leo
9	10°–00'–00"	Sag	Pis	Gem	Vir
10	11°–06'–40"	Cap	Ari	Can	Lib
11	12°–13'–20"	Aqu	Tau	Leo	Sco
12	13°–20'–00"	Pis	Gem	Vir	Sag
13	14°–26'–40"	Ari	Can	Lib	Cap

Saptvimshamsha (D27) Divisions					
Part	Degrees	Fiery (1,5,9)	Earthy (2,6,10)	Airy (3,7,11)	Watery (4,8,12)
14	15°–33'–20"	Tau	Leo	Sco	Aqu
15	16°–40'–00"	Gem	Vir	Sag	Pis
16	17°–46'–40"	Can	Lib	Cap	Ari
17	18°–53'–20"	Leo	Sco	Aqu	Tau
18	20°–00'–00"	Vir	Sag	Pis	Gem
19	21°–06'–40"	Lib	Cap	Ari	Can
20	22°–13'–20"	Sco	Aqu	Tau	Leo
21	23°–20'–00"	Sag	Pis	Gem	Vir
22	24°–26'–40"	Cap	Ari	Can	Lib
23	25°–33'–20"	Aqu	Tau	Leo	Sco
24	26°–40'–00"	Pis	Gem	Vir	Sag
25	27°–46'–40"	Ari	Can	Lib	Cap
26	28°–53'–20"	Tau	Leo	Sco	Aqu
27	30°–00'–00"	Gem	Vir	Sag	Pis

Saptvimshamsha is seen for physical status.

This is the research area of author. This chart has never been seen in this field of medical astrology. We will discuss it in detail in the research chapter.

The Saptvimshamsha chart for example horoscope is given

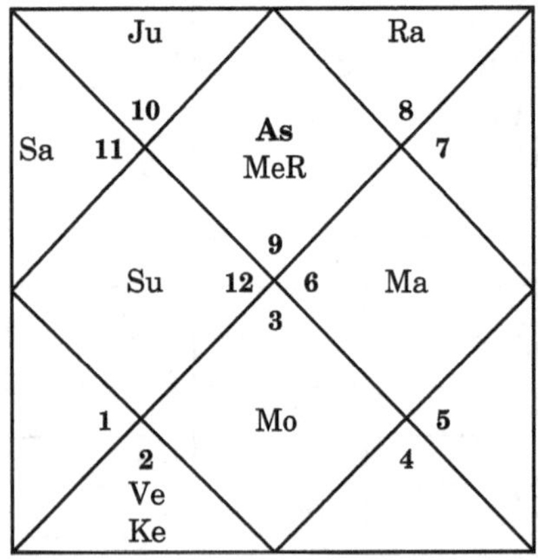

Su		Ve Ke	Mo
Sa	D27: Saptavim- -shamsha (Strength)		
Ju			
As MeR	Ra		Ma

Longitude of planets in D 27

The longitude of Lagna and the planets can be derived for the divisional charts. The principal behind it is "that a planet covers full sign of 30 degrees in one part of the divisional chart."

For example, each part of Dashamsha is of three degrees. In these three degrees of birth chart any planet covers one sign in Dashamsha. The longitude of a planet in Dashamsha is thus ten times of birth longitude. Two methods are given for working out the longitudes in divisional charts. These are applicable to all divisional charts except Parashar Trimshamsha.

First Method

Take the longitude of the Lagna or planets in the natal chart without the sign. The sign in D chart is already available.

Multiply these degree/min/seconds by the number of the divisional chart for which the longitude is being calculated. Leave the completed signs and retain the degree/minutes/seconds as the longitude of planet for the divisional chart.

For example, if Sun is 13 degree 04 minutes in any sign. We like to calculate the longitude of Sun in Saptvimshamsha. Multiply 13 degree 4 minutes by 27. We get 352 degrees and 48 minutes. From 352 degrees remove 330 degrees as eleven completed signs. The remainder is 22-degree 48 min. This is the longitude of Sun in Saptvimshamsha.

Second Method

Take the longitude of the planet in the natal chart without the sign call it A.

Note the longitude where the preceding division of the divisional chart has ended. Call it B. Subtract B from A and take the remainder.

Multiply the remainder by the number of divisional chart and the result will be the longitude of planet for the divisional chart.

For example, Longitude of Sun is 13 degrees 4 minutes. The preceding division ended at 12 degrees 13 minutes 20 seconds. Subtracting this from longitude of Sun we get 50 minutes 40 seconds. Multiply this by 27 and we get 22 degrees 48 minutes as longitude in D 27.

Trimshamsha

This chart, as the name suggests, is the one thirtieth division of a sign. Maharishi Parashar however divides the sign in five unequal parts ruled by five planets Mars, Saturn, Jupiter, Mercury and Venus. Sun and Moon are not presiding over any part.

The portion of each planet in any sign is Mars 5^0, Saturn 5^0, Jupiter 8^0, Mercury 7^0 and Venus 5^0. For planets or Lagna in odd signs, the order of ruler ship is as given above. For planets in even sign, the order is reversed. For odd signs the planet occupies the odd sign of the lord of Trimshamsha where for even sign it occupies the even sign of the lord of Trimshamsha.

A table for casing of Trimshamsha is given.

Table for Odd Sign				
Part	Degrees	Lord	Sign in D30	Tatva
1	0° — 5°	Mars	Aries	Fire – Agni
2	5° — 10°	Saturn	Aquarius	Ari – Vayu
3	10° — 18°	Jupiter	Sagittarius	Ether – Akash
4	18° — 25°	Mercury	Gemini	Earth – Prithvi
5	25° — 30°	Venus	Libra	Water – Jala

Table for Even Sign				
Part	**Degrees**	**Lord**	**Sign in D30**	**Tatva**
1	0° — 5°	Venus	Taurus	Water – Jala
2	5° — 12°	Mercury	Virgo	Earth – Prithvi
3	12° — 20°	Jupiter	Pisces	Ether – Akash
4	20° — 25°	Saturn	Capricorn	Ari – Vayu
5	25° — 30°	Mars	Scorpio	Fire – Agni

Trimshamsha indicates the six weaknesses which a person can acquire. These are given by the planets rising in Trimshamsha chart. These are Anger (Mars), Greed (Rahu), intoxication (Saturn), Lust (Venus), jealousy (Mercury) and illusion (Ketu).

Look for a planet which is in Lagna or aspecting Lagna in Rashi chart. Now, if the Lagna of Trimshamsha belongs to that planet, then this planet is the cause of problem. In addition, if the same planet is in Trimshamsha Lagna or aspects it, then it is worst. We should look to the placement of sixth lord/and eighth lord of the natal chart to find the source of problem.

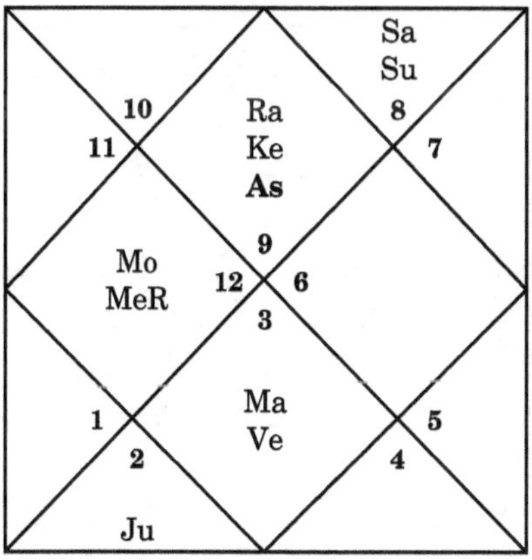

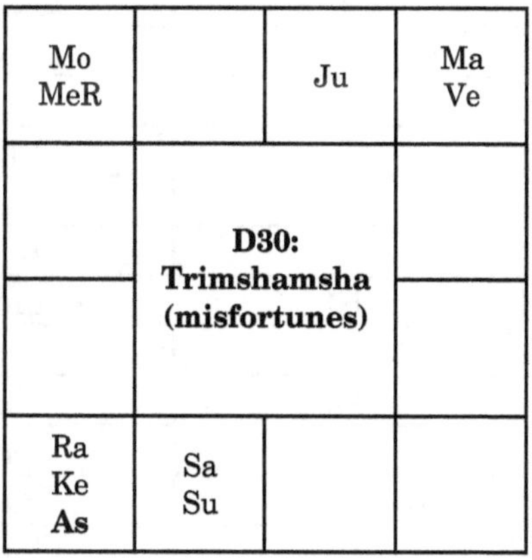

D30: Trimshamsha (misfortunes)			
Mo MeR		Ju	Ma Ve
	D30: Trimshamsha (misfortunes)		
Ra Ke As	Sa Su		

Relation of Planet, Tatva and Senses			
Planet	**Deity**	**Physical Tatva**	**Sense**
Mars	Agni	Fire	Sight
Saturn	Vayu	Air	Touch
Jupiter	Indra	Ether	Hearing
Mercury	Kuber	Earth	Smell
Venus	Varun	Water	Speech

Trimshamsha cyclical

In this method of casting of Trimshamsha we take thirty divisions of a sign. This gives better results for physical problems.

Table for this Trimshamsha is given.

Ending Longitude in a sign	Sign occupied in Trishamsha	
Degrees	**Odd Signs**	**Even Signs**
1	Aries	Libra
2	Taurus	Scorpio
3	Gemini	Sagittarius
4	Cancer	Capricorn
5	Leo	Aquarius
6	Virgo	Pisces
7	Libra	Aries
8	Scorpio	Taurus
9	Sagittarius	Gemini
10	Capricorn	Cancer
11	Aquarius	Leo
12	Pisces	Virgo
13	Aries	Libra
14	Taurus	Scorpio
15	Gemini	Sagittarius
16	Cancer	Capricorn
17	Leo	Aquarius

Ending Longitude in a sign	Sign occupied in Trishamsha	
Degrees	Odd Signs	Even Signs
18	Virgo	Pisces
19	Libra	Aries
20	Scorpio	Taurus
21	Sagittarius	Gemini
22	Capricorn	Cancer
23	Aquarius	Leo
24	Pisces	Virgo
25	Aries	Libra
26	Taurus	Scorpio
27	Gemini	Sagittarius
28	Cancer	Capricorn
29	Leo	Aquarius
30	Virgo	Pisces

Chapter 5

General

This chapter discusses the standard classical approach for identification of disease. The new research approach is given in another chapter.

What is disease?

Lack of ease is disease. This unease can be physical, mental, or emotional. Ayurveda assign this occurrence of disease to tri dosha. In astrology we have planets, houses, and signs. Thus, when any of the parameter is afflicted or is under malefic influence then disease is caused.

The area of disease is identified with astrological parameters. These analyses can be promise of disease and the time of occurrence. The timing is possible with running dasha and the promise is seen from the horoscope and divisional charts.

Four factors

Understanding disease is approached in four factors,

1. Diagnosis

2. Severity of disease (outcome)

3. Treatment

4. Timing (onset)

1. **Diagnosis.** The nature of disease and the location of disease come under diagnosis of disease. Medical practitioner gets the location of disease from patient

and reach conclusion about nature of disease by conducting tests etc. An astrologer gets the diagnosis from horoscope. This has been a weak area for an astrologer. **This book gives the method of diagnosis of disease with good reliability.**

2. **Severity of disease.** Every patient is worried about the seriousness of disease. The big question is the concern about the final outcome of disease. He is also worried about duration of illness. A good astrologer can well predict about the severity and duration of illness. Medical practitioners are equally competent to assess this area of disease.

3. **Treatment.** This is a weak area for astrologer. Very few astrologers are competent to suggest remedies and cure a disease. The medical science is very advanced in this area.

4. **Timing.** An astrologer can predict the onset and duration of disease in advance. Sometimes the symptoms of disease are not even present, but astrologer can predict the time of disease. Medical practitioner cannot foresee it.

Important discussion

The analysis of any horoscope normally is the examination of house, house lord and karaka. In common terms we say that a house is strong or weak. Let us understand how they become strong or weak. Also, we must know the difference in the role of house and house lord. House signifies certain matters, and these matters are solely indicated by the house.

House lord is the manager of the house and is responsible for upkeep of the house. If house lord is with malefic association, then he cannot look after the house. He will rather destroy the house. Now we must understand as to how the assessment of house and house lord is made.

A house is beneficial and capable of giving its results when it is associated or aspected by,

1.   House lord

2.   Lagna lord

3.   Benefic planets

4.   Karaka of house

5.   Subh kartari

A house lord is capable of managing its house when it is associated or aspected by,

1.   Benefic planets. Lord of lagna is always benefic

2.   Associated with lagna

3.   Lagna lord

4.   Karaka

5.   Subh kartari

Promise

The indicators of promise of disease or sound health are:

1.   Lagna and lagna lord.

2.   Moon.

3.   Houses of disease.

4.   Other factors.

1.   Lagna and Lagna lord

Lagna is the indicator of body. A strong lagna is a must for healthy body. The proneness to disease is dependent on the lagna. A weak lagna is prone to illness and a strong lagna is a safe guard against disease.

Lagna lord is the controller of lagna. It indicates the manner in which the person takes care of his body. A strong and well connected lagna lord is capable of warding off diseases. It should be well placed in Kendra trikona or eleventh house. A badly placed and afflicted lagna lord is not helpful to contain the disease. Even a debilitate lagna lord will protect provided it is well placed and have good association and aspect. Kartari yoga on lagna indicate dependence on the factors indicated by the planets causing kartari.

2.   Moon

Moon is the seed of strength of all planets. Moon is the mental strength or weakness. A Moon without any affliction is a provider of good mental support to sound health. Moon or mind governs body. Moon should be well placed and aspected. Ill placed moon is not welcome. Placement of Moon in trik houses is not considered good.

This placement gets worst when this Moon is associated or aspected by Malefic. Even when Moon is placed in Kendra with only Malefic occupying Kendra's can give disease. Papa kartari on Moon is like malefic association.

3.   Houses of disease

The trik houses are generally considered as giver of disease. We can broadly say that planets in trik houses, lords of trik houses, houses and planets having association or aspects are the giver of disease. Even malefic in Kendra can induce disease. The sixth sign of natural zodiac Virgo is also giver of disease.

Sixth house is the primary house of disease. The classics describe this house as house of Sadhna. Sadhna is the will to fight or achieve something. This can be a fight with illness.

Eighth house gives suddenness. This house also represents chronic disease. This house is known as Samadhi.

Twelfth house is expenditure or loss. This house is known as Vyaya.

We can summarize the disease givers as under.

a.   Planets placed in sixth house.

b.   Planets placed in eighth house.

c.   Planets placed in twelfth house.

d.   Lord of sixth house.

e.   Planets with sixth lord.

f.   Planets occupying the Navamsha of sixth lord or are with sixth lord in Navamsha.

g.   Planets aspected by sixth lord.

h.   Planets in Virgo sign. Lord of Virgo.

i.   The karaka of disease are Mars and Ketu.

j.   Malefic in Kendra.

4.   Other factors

Other considerations which can cause disease are,

1.   Planets in Mrityu Bhaga.

2.   Gulika and mandi.

3.   Chidra Graha

4.   Vish Navamsha.

5.   Sarp Drekkana.

6.   Bala Rishta.

These factors are also considered for timing of disease.

1.   Planets in Mrityu Bhaga (MB)

Mrityu Bhaga is the term used when a planet occupies certain degrees in a sign. These degrees are individual for each planet including lagna and Mandi.

Table for Mrityu Bhaga

Sign	Sun	Mon	Mar	Mer	Jup	Ven	Sat	Rah	Ket	Man	Lag
Aries	20	26	19	15	19	28	10	14	8	23	1
Taurus	9	12	28	14	29	15	4	13	18	24	9
Gemini	12	13	25	13	12	11	7	12	20	11	22
Cancer	6	25	23	12	27	17	9	11	10	12	22
Leo	8	24	29	8	6	10	12	24	21	13	25
Virgo	24	11	28	18	4	13	16	23	22	14	2
Libra	16	26	14	20	13	4	3	22	23	8	4
Scorpio	17	14	21	10	10	6	18	21	24	18	23
Sagittarius	22	13	2	21	17	27	28	10	11	20	18
Capricorn	2	25	15	22	11	12	14	20	12	10	20
Aquarius	3	5	11	7	15	29	13	18	13	21	24
Pisces	23	12	6	5	28	19	15	8	14	22	10

It will be very rare that any planet, lagna or mandi will be on exact degrees of MB. A range within which any planet is considered in MB is given,

a. The longitude of lagna, Moon or Mercury should be within +/- 40 min of degree of MB.

b. Sun should be within +/- 20 min of the MB degree.

c. Rest of them should be within +/-15 min of the MB degree in MB.

d. Any planet in MB affects the house significations where it is placed and the house which it lords.

e. It affects the natural significations of the planet.

f. It also passes its influence to the lord of house where it is placed.

Any benefic association with the planet in MB will lessen the ill effect but the malefic association will aggravate the ill effects. Aspect of Jupiter on the planet in MB is a great relief.

The dasha periods of the following planets can be serious.

a.   Dasha of a planet in MB

b.   Maha dasha or antar dasha of the lord of the house which contains the planet in MB.

c.   Antar dasha of the planet who is associated or aspected by planet in MB.

d.   These malefic periods become more serious when two malefic transits over the natal position of planet in MB.

2.   Gulika and Mandi

These are malefic Upgraha of Saturn. Most scholars use them in predictive astrology as without any difference. Sarvarth Chintamani says that Gulika represent Saturn and Mandi represent Yama as upgraha.

The major difference is in the method of calculation.

a.   Mandi

Mandi is calculated separately for day and night. For a day birth we calculate day mandi and for a night birth we calculate night mandi. The classics have given the time of birth of mandi from Sun rise or Sun set. The basic assumptions are,

1.   The duration of day and night is equal and each is of 30 Ghati.

2.   The time of birth of mandi depends on the week day.

3.   The time of birth is from Sun rise for day mandi and is from Sun set for night mandi.

A table for time of birth of mandi for different week days is given in Ghati.

Week day	Time of birth in ghati for day	Time of birth in ghati for night
Sunday	26	10
Monday	22	6
Tuesday	18	2
Wednesday	14	26
Thursday	10	22
Friday	6	18
Saturday	2	14

The step-by-step method is given.

1. Decide which mandi is required to be calculated. It is day mandi or night mandi.

2. Note the Sun rise or Sun set time in standard time at the place of calculation. Sun rise for day mandi and Sun set for night mandi.

3. Note the time of birth of mandi from the table given.

4. Convert this time interval from Ghati to hours and minutes.

5. Add this interval to the time of Sun rise or Sun set as the case may be.

6. The time so arrived is the time of birth of mandi.

7. Work out the ascendant rising at the time of birth of mandi. The date and place is known to us.

8. The ascendant so arrived is the longitude of mandi.

This mandi is arrived with the condition that the duration of day and night is equal to 30 Ghati each. It is not so always. We have to adjust this time of birth of mandi proportionally according to actual duration of day and night.

b.   Gulika

Method of calculation of Gulika takes the duration of day and night at the place of birth. A step-by-step method is given.

1.   Decide which Gulika is required to be calculated. It is day Gulika or night Gulika.

2.   Note the Sun rise or Sun set time in standard time at the place of calculation.

3.   Work out duration of day for day Gulika (Sun set – Sun rise).

4.   Work out duration of night for night Gulika (Sun rise – Sun set).

5.   Divide this duration of day or night, as required, in eight equal parts.

6.   The first part in day belongs to the week day. The first part in night belongs to the fifth day from the week day.

7.   The next part is the next week day from first part week day both in day or in night. For example, if first part is Tuesday than second will be of Wednesday and so on.

8.   The ending point of the part belonging to Saturn is the time of birth of Gulika.

Any planet with Gulika brings bad according to its natural significations and lordship of the planet. The lord of sign occupied by Gulika also suffers.

3.   Chidra Graha

These are planets connected with eighth house. There are seven Chidra Graha. These are,

a.   Lord of eighth house.

b.   Planets placed in eighth house.

c.   Planets aspecting eighth house.

d.   Planets conjoined with eighth lord.

e.   Bitter enemy of eighth lord.

f.   Lord of 22nd Drekkana from lagna.

g.   Lord of 64th Navamsha from Moon.

When a Chidra Graha is afflicted, it can become a maraca. A benefic association or aspect will reduce the malefic effect. A troubled Chidra Graha can give disease in its dasha.

4.   **Vish Navamsha**

Certain Navamsha position of planets is termed as Vish Navamsha. These are,

a.   First Navamsha of Aries, Taurus, Virgo and Sagittarius. These are also called Sarp Navamsha.

b.   Fifth Navamsha of Gemini, Leo, Libra and Aquarius. These are also called gridha Navamsha.

c.   Ninth Navamsha of Cancer, Scorpio, Capricorn and Pisces. These are also called shookar Navamsha.

Any planet placed in these Navamsha is harmful to the relative signified by the planet. If Moon occupies any of these Navamsha then it brings harm to mother.

5.   **Sarp Drekkana**

Certain Drekkana position of planets is termed as Sarp Drekkana. These are,

a.   Second and third Drekkana of Cancer.

b.   First and second Drekkana of Scorpio.

c.   Third Drekkana of Pisces.

Planets placed in these Drekkana bring misfortune in their dasha periods. Even planets associated or aspected by these can bring harm.

6. Balarishta

Balarishta is the term used for the arishta in childhood and up to the age of 12 years. The arishta in the first four years is due to past life karmas of mother. The arishta from four to eight years are due to past life karmas of father and from eight to twelve years is the result of past life karma of the child.

Balarishta not necessarily means death. It can cause agony in any form.

1. Moon placed in a trik house and aspected by Malefic.

2. Moon is placed in Nakshatra Gandanta and is associated or aspected by Malefic.

3. Moon and all Malefic are placed in Kendra.

4. Weak Moon is placed in lagna and Malefic in Kendra and the eighth house.

5. Moon in lagna and malefic in seventh house.

6. Moon is hemmed between Malefic and without benefic aspect.

7. A retrograde benefic in a trik house and aspected by Benefics.

8. Birth at the time of Sun set or Sun rise in the hora of Moon and the Moon is in Rashi gandanta.

9. When Cancer or Scorpio is rising and all malefic in tenth to fourth house and Benefics from fourth to tenth house. This is called Vajra Mushti yoga.

10. Birth is at the time of an eclipse and Mars or Saturn aspects lagna.

11. Mars, Sun and Saturn are together in eighth or sixth house.

12. Malefic in sixth or eighth house and aspected by malefic.

13. A weak Moon in twelfth house and Malefic in lagna and eighth house with no Benefics in Kendra.

Note: When a Balarishta combination is present in the horoscope and any one of the following is the placement of planets, then Balarishta gains strength.

a. Sun in fifth house (some say twelfth house)

b. Moon in first, sixth, eight or twelfth house.

c. Mars in seventh house.

d. Mercury in fourth house (some say seventh house)

e. Jupiter in third house.

f. Venus in sixth house.

g. Saturn in lagna.

h. Rahu in ninth house.

I. Ketu in twelfth house.

Cancellation of Arishta

1. A strong Jupiter placed in lagna.

2. All Benefics occupy Kendra position.

3. Strong lagna lord placed in Kendra and aspected by benefic.

4. Moon is in trik house for a birth in day time in Krishna paksha or a night birth in Shukla paksha.

5. Moon occupies any sign of Venus, Mercury or Jupiter in Drekkana or in Navamsha.

6.   Rahu in third, sixth or eleventh house and aspected by a benefic.

7.   Rahu placed in lagna in Aries or Taurus or Cancer.

8.   All planets occupy sheershodaya signs.

9.   A strong benefic is placed in Kendra.

10.   Bright Moon aspected by all planets.

11.   Benefics in trik houses from lagna or Moon and not associated with malefic.

12.   Jupiter in own sign or exalted and placed in Kendra or Trikona.

Chapter 6

Classical Combinations

Classical Combinations for Diseases are taken from various books. These are the basic starting reference for locating and identifying the diseases. It should be applied liberally and not literally.

Good Health

1.   Lagna lord is in his exaltation sign or in own sign or in the sign of a friend in Navamsha or is Vargottam and is associated or aspected by a benefic.

2.   Lagna lord is in Kendra or in trine and not associated or aspected by malefic.

3.   Benefics in Kendra and trines without malefic aspect.

4.   A benefic sign rises in lagna and is not afflicted by any malefic.

5.   Jupiter is in lagna or aspects lagna.

6.   Moon sign lord and the eleventh lord are conjoined.

7.   Lord of Navamsha lagna is in a watery sign and the sign in lagna is a benefic sign.

8.   Lagna lord is in watery sign and a watery planet (Moon or Venus) is in lagna or aspects it.

9.   Lagna lord is in watery sign and Jupiter or Mercury is in lagna or aspects it from a watery sign.

10. No malefic is placed in Kendra and eighth house. Jupiter and lagna lord are in Kendra. The person lives for 100 years free from disease.

11. Benefics occupy Kendra, Trines, second house, eighth house, eleventh house and malefic occupy trishadaya houses.

12. Sun for a day birth, Moon for a night birth and placed in eleventh house wards off crores of evils.

13. When lord of ascendant is in own Navamsha associated or aspected by a benefic, sound health is assured.

14. When ascendant is occupied by its own lord, the sound health is assured.

Poor health/ sickly

1. Lagna lord with a malefic.

2. Lagna lord is in trik house. Any relation with malefic will certainly give poor health.

3. Lord of trik a house occupies lagna.

4. Eleventh lord in sixth house.

5. Sixth lord in eighth house.

6. Eighth lord in sixth house.

7. Lagna lord is combust or in enemy sign or debilitated without cancellation of debilitation.

8. Lords of trik houses occupy their own house and weak lagna lord is in trishadaya house.

9. Malefic is placed in lagna and lagna lord is weak.

10. Moon in lagna and afflicted by malefic.

11. Malefic are in Taurus or Libra and not aspected by Jupiter or Venus or Mars.

12. Moon is weak.

13. Malefic lagna lord is in lagna with Moon.

14. Lagna lord and sixth lord are in mutual aspect.

15. Lagna lord and eighth lord exchange sign and the lagna is afflicted by malefic.

Defect in body

1. Sun and Moon are in Kendra.

2. Malefic in Kendra without any benefic relation.

3. Saturn in second house, Moon in tenth house and Mercury in seventh house.

4. Sun in Libra and any one of Moon, Venus or Saturn is debilitated.

Long duration illness/ serious illness

1. Malefic is placed in sixth house, sixth lord is with a malefic and Saturn Rahu is conjoined.

2. Lagna lord is in sixth house, Moon in lagna and aspected by malefic.

3. Jupiter, Venus and lagna lord are combust and Moon is in sixth or eighth house.

4. Sun is in lagna, Moon is in sixth house and lagna lord fifth lord have malefic relation.

5. Moon is in eighth house and malefic in seventh, tenth and twelfth house.

6. Mars and Saturn are in lagna. Lagna lord in second, eighth or twelfth house and no benefic in Kendra.

7. Sixth lord is exalted.

8. Sixth lord is placed in lagna in a male sign.

Lean and thin

1. Lagna lord and Moon sign lord are placed in trik house.

2. Sun is in twelfth house and Mars is not in Kendra.

3. Saturn and Moon are in Aries.

4.   Depositor of lagna lord is in trik house.

5.   A dry sign (Aries, Taurus, Gemini, Leo, Virgo, Sagittarius) rises in lagna and has malefic relation.

6.   Lagna lord placed in dry sign.

7.   Lagna lord in the sign belonging to Sun or Mars or Saturn.

8.   Jupiter or Mercury in lagna in a dry sign.

9.   Dry planets (Sun, Mars, Saturn) in lagna in dry sign.

Pituitary Glands

It is located at the base of the brain. Venus is the planet which governs this gland. Afflicted Venus causes disease of Pituitary gland.

1.   Venus is placed in sixth house with a malefic.

2.   Venus is with sixth lord and placed in Aries or Virgo.

Brain

1.   Affliction to Sun causes brain disease.

2.   Aries represent head of a person and affliction to Aries and Mars cause head/ brain disease.

3.   When ascendant and the ascendant lord is afflicted.

4.   Saturn in eighth house with Mars in seventh house cause tumour.

5.   Afflicted Saturn in lagna cause tumour.

Epilepsy

1.   Moon and Rahu in eighth house.

2.   Sixth or eighth house afflicted by Saturn and Mars.

3.   Saturn and Moon are aspected by Mars.

4.   Sun, Moon and Mars conjoined in lagna or eighth house and afflicted by malefic.

5.   Moon in sixth house and Rahu in lagna.

6.   Birth at the time of eclipse with Jupiter in lagna or a trine and Saturn and Mars in sixth or eighth.

7.   Moon and Venus are in Kendra and malefic occupy fifth and eighth house. This yoga is called Mahagada yoga.

Migraine

1.   Mars in lagna and afflicted by malefic.

2.   Rahu under malefic influence in lagna.

3.   Mars and Moon are conjunct.

4.   Saturn in lagna as lagna lord and afflicted.

Meningitis

1.   Mercury afflicted in sixth house.

2.   Lagna and sixth lord in fifth house and aspected by Mars.

3.   Lagna under the influence of Rahu and Mars.

4.   Moon, fifth house and sixth house afflicted by Mars and Rahu.

Hysteria

1.   Association of Moon with Rahu or Ketu can make a person hysterical.

2.   Fourth house afflicted.

Mental Disease

1.   Weak Moon and Saturn are together in 12th house.

2.   Weak Moon and Saturn are together and are aspected by Mars.

3.   Moon conjoined with Rahu and aspected by Saturn.

4.   Mars in 4th house with Saturn or aspected by Saturn.

5.   Saturn in 4th house and aspected by Mars.

6.   Saturn in 4th house with Rahu or Ketu.

7.   Moon is with a malefic and Rahu is placed in fifth, eighth or twelfth house.

8.   Moon and Mercury are in Kendra's afflicted by malefic without any benefic relation or not aspected by the lord of the said sign will suffer insanity.

9.   Saturn, Mars and Moon are placed in Kendra's.

10. Sixth lord and Saturn are in Lagna.

11. Mars and Mercury in 6th or 8th house.

12. Mercury with a malefic is placed in 3rd, 6th, 8th or 12th house.

13. Mars is in 3rd house and is afflicted by a malefic.

14. Saturn and Rahu together in Virgo lagna.

15. Mars in lagna and Jupiter in seventh house or vice versa.

16. Saturn in lagna and Mars in fifth, seventh or ninth house.

17. Saturn in lagna, Sun in twelfth house and Mars or Moon in trine.

18. Saturn and lord of second house are associated with Sun or Mars.

19. Gulika in seventh or fifth house and afflicted by malefic.

20. Rahu and Moon in lagna and malefic in trines.

Loss of memory

1.   No benefic is in fifth house.

2.   Saturn, Rahu and Gulika are placed in fifth house.

3.   Fifth lord is with malefic or aspected by a malefic without any benefic association.

4.   Fifth lord is with a malefic and again associates with malefic in Shashtiamsha.

Mental derangement

1.   Jupiter is in lagna and Mars is in seventh house.

2.   Saturn is in lagna and Mars is in seventh house or in trines.

3.   Saturn in lagna, Sun in twelfth and Mars or Moon in trine.

4.   Birth is on Tuesday or Saturday. Sun and Moon are in lagna or trines or Saturn and Jupiter in Kendra.

5.   Moon and Mercury are in Kendra and are not in benefic Navamsha.

6.   Moon and Rahu in twelfth house and a malefic and a benefic in eighth house.

Mentally weak

1.   Moon and Saturn in lagna and Mars is in seventh house.

2.   Mars is hemmed between Sun and Moon.

3.   Mars and Moon in lagna and Mercury in seventh house.

4.   Mercury in lagna and Sun Saturn are in sixth house.

Ear disease

Third house is the house of communication. It denoted ears of a person. Mercury is the significator of hearing. Generally, 3rd house represent right ear and 11th house is the left ear.

Third house- Any malefic influence on the third house/ lord indicate defect in the ear or difficulty in hearing. More malefic influence indicates serious problem.

Eleventh house- Similar malefic influence on eleventh house can also cause defective hearing.

Karaka- afflicted Mercury without any influence of benefic can also give difficult hearing. Strong Mercury indicates a healthy ear and hearing.

Kaal Purush- Gemini is the third sign of natural zodiac and also represents ears. Affliction to Gemini is an indicator of ear disease.

When all these factors are under malefic influence it indicates complete deafness. Benefic influence will be a great relieving factor and give moderate problem.

1.   Mercury placed in a trik house and aspected by Saturn.

2.   Mercury is the sixth lord and Saturn aspects Mercury and sixth house.

3.   Mercury and sixth lord conjoined in a trik house and aspected by Saturn.

4.   Mercury is placed in 4th house from Saturn and 6th lord in a trik house.

5.   Malefic located in 3rd/ 9th or 5th/ 11th houses and without any benefic association or aspect.

6.   Mercury and Saturn in 12th house cause disease in left ear.

7.   Debilated Venus with Rahu is placed in any house in the chart.

8.   Mercury and sixth lord are placed in fourth house and Saturn is in lagna.

9.   Sun and Mercury conjunct in trishadaya and aspected by Mars and Saturn.

10.   Venus in Taurus in 6th house and a malefic Moon aspects Venus.

11.   Birth in night time with Venus in 5th house and Mercury in 6th house.

12.   Mercury, Mars and Moon conjunct in 3rd or 9th house in Rahu/ Ketu axis.

13.   Second lord in lagna with Mars and Saturn, The ear of person is cut.

14.   Second lord and sixth lord in lagna and Gulika with Mars in eighth house then also the person loose his ear.

15.   Saturn in 3rd house with Gulika gives nervous trouble in ear.

16.   Third lord occupy a malefic Shashtiamsha.

17.   Mars as sixth or eighth lord conjoin Sun in third, ninth, eleventh, sixth or twelfth house and do not have association or aspect of benefic.

18.   Third house is occupied by malefic and Gulika.

19.   Mercury and Venus in twelfth house.

Total Deafness

1.   Moon occupy lagna, third house or eleventh house and is conjoined and aspected by malefic.

2.   Malefic occupy fifth and ninth house and also aspected by malefic.

3.   Mercury is in fourth house from Saturn and sixth lord is in a trik house.

4.   Full Moon and Venus are with malefic.

5.   Mercury and sixth lord are aspected by malefic.

6.   Jupiter, third house and eleventh house afflicted.

Dumb and deaf

1.   Mercury occupies any one of dumb signs (Cancer, Scorpio, and Pisces) and is aspected by Moon of Amavasya.

2.   Mercury and sixth lord are in lagna.

3.   Jupiter and sixth lord are in lagna.

4.   Jupiter and sixth lord are in trik house.

Eye Disease

Venus is the prime significator of vision in the eye. Sun and Moon are the right and left eye respectively. Second house is right eye and twelfth house is left eye. Taurus and Pisces is the second and twelfth house of natural zodiac and thus represent the right and left eye respectively. The extent of damage to eyes is decided by the severity of affliction to significator or houses/ signs. It can be from total blindness to minor eye disease.

Good eyesight

1.   Benefics are placed in second house.

2.   Second lord is associated with Benefics.

3.   Sun is with lagna lord or is aspected by lagna lord.

4.   Lord of twelfth house is with a benefic, is in benefic Navamsha and is influenced by benefic.

5.   Second lord and twelfth lords are strong in Shadbal.

Total Blindness

In the following combinations if there is a benefic association then it is defective or poor eye sight and total blindness is not present.

1.   Sun and Moon in twelfth house and afflicted by malefic.

2.   Sun and Moon in lagna which is identical with Aries, Cancer or Leo and are aspected by Mars and Saturn. Even when only Saturn aspects then it give blindness also.

3.   Mars in second house, Saturn in twelfth house, Moon in sixth house and Sun in eighth house.

4.   Sun and Moon are in eighth house with Saturn in sixth or twelfth house for Pisces or Libra lagna.

5.   Heavily afflicted Sun in Libra.

6.   Sun and Rahu in lagna, Mars and Saturn in fifth or ninth house. (Malefic in trines)

7.   Venus and lord of ascendant are in a trik house along with second and twelfth lords.

8.   Mars is the second lord, Sun and Moon are in eighth house, and Saturn is in sixth or twelfth house.

9.   Lords of second, twelfth house and Venus are in trik house.

10.   Lord of lagna, Sun and Venus are placed in trik house.

11.   Sun and Moon are conjoined and the second lord is in trik house.

12.   Mars in second house, Moon in sixth house, Sun in eighth house and Saturn in twelfth house.

13.   Afflicted Moon in second house from Sun.

14.   Moon in sixth house for Gemini lagna and associated or aspected by malefic.

15.   Mars is combust in lagna.

16.   Sun and Moon together in a Kendra and occupy Aquarius in Navamsha.

17.   Moon in lagna and occupy Aries, Taurus or Cancer in Navamsha.

18.   Moon in lagna at 20-degree Pisces or 19-degree Taurus.

19.   Lord of lagna in a malefic sign in eighth house.

20.   Mars occupy sixth house from Moon.

21.   Moon and Venus in second house and afflicted by malefic.

22.   Sun is conjoined with lords of lagna and second house.

23. Lagna lord, second lord and Venus are placed in exaltation sign, Mooltrikona sign or Navamsha sign of Venus.

24. Sun, Venus, lagna lord and second lord in trik house.

25. Two malefic occupy fourth and fifth house. Moon is in a trik house without any benefic relation.

Blind in one eye

1. When lord of ninth house is placed in Aries or Leo or Scorpio or Capricorn and

2. Moon is in Leo and Mars is in Aquarius.

3. Sun is in Cancer and Mars is in Capricorn

4. Moon and Mars are in lagna and are aspected by Venus and Jupiter.

5. Moon and Sun are in sixth and twelfth house. Husband and wife both are one eyed.

Squint

1. Second lord is exalted in Navamsha and is conjoined with Venus.

2. Second lord is in the sign of Venus and is aspected or associated with lagna lord.

Eye Disease

1. Sun and Moon are afflicted by Saturn and Mars.

2. Saturn and Mars in sixth or eighth house.

3. Sun in lagna in Cancer and aspected by malefic.

4. Sun or Moon in lagna or seventh house with Saturn or Rahu.

5. Sun and/ or Moon in trik house.

6. Sun and/ or Moon in trik house with Saturn or Mars.

7.   Lord of lagna with lord or second or twelfth houses are placed in trik house.

8.   Venus is with fifth and sixth lord.

9.   Saturn and Mars afflict second lord and are placed in second house.

10. Sun, Moon and Venus are in trik houses.

11. Sun is placed in eighth house.

12. Moon and Mars occupy same Navamsha.

13. Sun in fifth or ninth or twelfth house and associated or aspected by malefic the gets sore eyes.

14. Moon and Venus in second house with malefic.

15. Lord of sixth house or Moon is with malefic and placed in dark half of horoscope then a spot is present in the eye.

16. Waning Moon is aspected by Saturn but not aspected by Venus, the eyes are small.

17. Moon is in Cancer and is aspected by a malefic from seventh or tenth house, the eyes are small.

18. Venus is placed in lagna or in eighth house and aspected by malefic then eyes will be full of tears.

19. Two malefic in second house.

20. Moon in second house and afflicted by malefic.

21. For Aquarius lagna, Moon is in the sign of a retrograde planet.

22. Moon in sixth house without any benefic association or aspect.

23. Venus as sixth lord is in lagna and a retrograde benefic in trik house.

24. Second lord and twelfth lord together in trik house from Venus.

25.　　Lagna lord with malefic and aspected by Saturn.

26.　　Second lord is with Saturn or Mars or Gulika.

27.　　Lord of Navamsha sign of second lord is in sign of a malefic or is with a malefic.

28.　　Sun is conjoined with Gulika and aspected by Mars.

29.　　Lords of Navamsha of tenth lord and sixth lord are in trik house along with lagna lord. The second lord and Venus occupy eighth house then there is **serious trouble** in the eyes.

30.　　Sun, Moon and Venus together in any house.

31.　　Sun, Venus and lord of lagna are in the invisible half.

Weak or defective eye

1.　　Mars or Mercury is approaching Sun.

2.　　Mars and Moon are in same sign or in same Navamsha then there is mark in the eye.

3.　　Moon and sixth lord are with malefic in the invisible half.

4.　　Weak Moon is aspected by Saturn and not by Venus.

5.　　Lagna lord is in third, sixth or eighth house and is aspected by Mars or Mercury.

6.　　Moon in Cancer and is aspected by a malefic placed in seventh or tenth house.

7.　　Second lord or twelfth lord is placed in trik house from Venus.

8.　　Sun in fifth, ninth or twelfth house and aspected by malefic.

9.　　Lagna lord and eighth lord in sixth house give defect in left eye.

10.　　Venus in sixth house gives defect in right eye.

11.   Second lord or twelfth lord is in sixth house and Venus
       in lagna or eighth house and afflicted by malefic.

Redness of eyes

1.   Second lord is with Mars and Sun or is aspected by
      them.

Cataract

1.   Sun with Ketu in second house or in a trik house gives
      cataract.

2.   Afflicted Sun in lagna in a watery sign.

3.   Mars in lagna and Ketu in second house.

Night Blindness

1.   Sun and Moon are in second house.

2.   Sun in Libra and is in lagna.

3.   Sun in Leo and afflicted by malefic.

4.   Moon and Venus are placed in trik house.

5.   Venus, Moon and second lord are in lagna. If benefic
      associates or any of these is in exaltation then blindness
      is not present.

6.   Moon in second house with Venus or malefic.

Loss of eye

1.   Sun and Moon are in lagna and aspected by Mars and
      Saturn. When a benefic is associated then loss of eye is
      not there.

2.   Lords of tenth and sixth house are debilitated in
      Navamsha and occupy lagna with a malefic planet and
      Venus and second lord.

3.   Moon and Venus are in seventh or twelfth house
      indicate loss of left eye.

Digestive System

Venus is the Karaka of digestion. Sixth house and Virgo are the house and sign representing the stomach. Sun is the karaka of bowels. Affliction to these when caused by Mars or Mercury then it is tumors and ulcers. Rahu causes tuberculosis of bowels. Ketu is responsible for pains.

1. Moon in sixth house or in Virgo sign cause indigestion. Any association or aspect of a malefic with such Moon cause bowel irregularity and disturbs intestinal function.

2. Saturn in lagna, sixth or eighth house is conjoined with a luminary cause food poisoning.

3. Mars in lagna and sixth lord is weak.

4. Malefic Rahu in lagna or trik house cause indigestion.

5. Saturn in lagna causes indigestion.

6. Malefic in lagna and Saturn in eighth house cause bowel disease.

7. Lagna lord, second lord and fourth lord conjoined cause cholera and stomach disease.

8. Sun in lagna in birth chart or in Navamsha with Moon, Mercury and Rahu in Leo cause bowel disorder.

9. Sixth lord and Lagna lord are in lagna and Mars in own sign give stomach disorder.

10. A malefic in sixth house and sixth lord in seventh house with a malefic also gives stomach problems.

11. Sixth lord in third house cause abdominal problems.

12. Rahu or Ketu in lagna.

13. Saturn in eighth house and Moon in lagna.

Diarrhea

1.   Rahu and Mercury in lagna with Mars and Saturn in seventh house.

2.   Moon and Venus are placed in eighth house.

3.   Mars, Saturn and Rahu conjoined.

Dysentery

1.   Venus is placed in seventh house with a malefic.

2.   Mars and Venus in eighth house.

3.   Rahu and Saturn in second house in birth chart or in Navamsha lagna.

4.   Lagna lord occupy Pisces in Navamsha and is PAC malefic.

Piles

1.   Saturn in lagna and Mars in seventh house.

2.   Saturn is aspected by malefic.

3.   Sun in lagna, Saturn in eighth and Mars in Scorpio.

4.   Mars and lagna lord in seventh house and Saturn in twelfth house.

5.   Saturn in twelfth house and aspected by Mars and lagna lord.

6.   Lagna lord occupy sign of Mars or Mercury and afflicted by malefic lead to anal disease.

Abscess

1.   Moon is in papa kartari and Sun in Capricorn.

2.   Moon is in papa kartari and Saturn in seventh house.

Cancer abdomen

1.   Rahu or Ketu in lagna with a malefic sixth lord.

2.   Rahu or Ketu in eighth or twelfth house and the sixth house is afflicted.

Nervous System (Epilepsy, neurasthenia, hysteria)

Mercury is the significator of nerves. Affliction to mercury is the root cause of diseases of nerves. The nerve control is brain which is represented by lagna and the sign Aries.

1.   Moon and Mercury in Kendra and aspected by a malefic and malefic is placed in fifth or eighth house.

2.   Moon and Mercury in Kendra and all malefic in eighth house.

3.   Moon and Mercury in fifth house and all malefic in eighth house.

4.   Moon in trik house with any of Rahu or Ketu or Saturn or Mars.

5.   Moon, Mars and Sun in lagna or eighth house and aspected by Saturn.

6.   Moon with Rahu in lagna and malefic in trines.

7.   Moon with Rahu or Saturn and Mercury is weak.

Paralysis

Mercury is the ruler if nerves and Saturn is the ruler of muscles. The extremities suffer in the paralytic stroke. The right leg is ruled by second house and the left leg by twelfth house. Right hand is ruled by third house and left hand by eleventh house.

1.   Saturn is placed in an airy sign and Mercury is afflicted.

2.   Moon and Mercury join Rahu or Saturn.

Teeth

1.   Saturn is the significator of teeth and Rahu is the giver of dental disease.

Defective teeth

1. Saturn in second house gives defective teeth.

2. Rahu in lagna or in second house. In second house gives big teeth.

3. Ketu in lagna.

4. Saturn and Rahu in lagna or second house.

5. Sun, Moon and Saturn in seventh house destroys teeth.

Teeth disease

1. Malefic Saturn in Cancer.

2. Any malefic in seventh house without any benefic association.

3. Lagna is any one of Aries, Taurus or Sagittarius sign and is aspected by a malefic.

4. The Navamsha lagna is a sign of Saturn.

5. Second lord and Rahu are placed in a trik house.

6. Second lord and depositor of Rahu are together in a trik house. (Disease sets in the Sub period of Rahu or second lord)

7. Second lord and sixth lord associated with malefic.

8. Rahu or Ketu is placed in sixth house. It also gives lip disease.

9. Rahu in lagna or fifth house.

10. Jupiter and Rahu in lagna.

11. If the lord of Navamsha of the planet which is lord of Navamsha of second lord is associated with sixth lord.

12. Moon in fourth house with Gulika and occupy Cancer, Scorpio or Aquarius sign in Navamsha.

13. For Capricorn lagna, Venus is in ninth house with a malefic and aspected by a malefic.

14.   Seventh lord in fourth house.

Nose

Second house rules nose of a person. The airy signs control the breathing. Rahu is the significator of the action of breathing. Mercury is the significator of nose and affliction to Mercury causes disease of nose and breathing.

1.   Mercury is conjoined with a malefic or aspected by a malefic but without any malefic association or aspect.

2.   Moon, Saturn and a malefic in trik house and lord of lagna in malefic Navamsha.

3.   Second house and lord are afflicted with Moon in sixth house and lagna lord in malefic Navamsha.

4.   Jupiter as sixth lord afflicts second house.

5.   Mars, Saturn and Moon conjoined and related to second lord or Mercury.

Mouth

1.   For Gemini lagna Moon is related to second house.

2.   Mars, Saturn and Mercury in lagna.

3.   Mercury afflicted in second house.

Tongue

Second house rules over tongue and speech. Jupiter is the significator. Taurus is the second house of natural zodiac. All signs of watery trine are mute signs.

Defective speech

1.   Weak Mercury in second house and under aspect of malefic.

2.   Lagna lord and second lord occupy malefic Navamsha then there is nervous trouble in organ of speech.

3.   A weak second lord under aspect of malefic give defective speech.

Dumb

1. Moon is in Gandanta and Jupiter is placed in trik house.

2. Second lord and Jupiter in ninth house or a trik house.

Tongue disease

1. Second lord in a trik house with Rahu or depositor of Rahu.

2. Jupiter placed in a trik house.

Ear

Second house rules outer ear and third house rules inner ear. Jupiter is the significator of ears and hearing. All signs of airy trine control hearing.

1. Mars or Rahu with malefic in third house.

2. Any malefic in third house and aspected by a malefic.

3. Third lord heavily afflicted.

4. Malefic in third, fifth, ninth and eleventh house without any benefic relation.

5. Second or third lord in lagna with malefic.

6. Seventh lord in lagna with Mars and the second and third house afflicted.

7. Malefic influence on eleventh lord.

8. Venus with Rahu in ninth house then loss of ear.

Throat

Third house rules the throat and Gemini is the third house of natural zodiac. Venus is the significator of throat.

1. Third lord placed with Mercury.

2. Third house occupied by a malefic and aspected by a malefic.

3. A malefic and Gulika is placed in third house.

4.   Lord of second and third house with Rahu.

5.   Mars and Saturn in sixth or twelfth house along with lord of third house.

Tonsil

Placement of lagna lord in a trik house with any other planet gives problem of tonsils due various reasons.

1.   With Moon- Due to water

2.   With Mars- Hard lumps

3.   With Mercury- Pitta

4.   With Jupiter- Mucus

5.   With Venus- TB of throat.

Chest and lungs

Fourth house represent chest and lungs. Cancer is the fourth sign of natural zodiac. Jupiter governs lungs. Sun and Moon are significator of chest. Rahu is the main afflicter and cause disease when it afflicts fourth house or cancer. The source of infection due to various planets are, Mercury- school, Venus- women, Sun- home or family, Saturn- labor, Mars- co born or battle field, Moon- water.

Tuberculosis

1.   Libra rises in lagna and Sun and Jupiter are placed in sixth house.

2.   Sun is placed in lagna and is aspected by Mars. (it can give trouble of spleen)

3.   Watery sign in sixth or eighth house and any one of Jupiter, Sun or Venus is afflicted by malefic in that house.

4.   Rahu, Ketu or Saturn in eighth house conjoined with maraca and malefic.

5.   Jupiter or lagna in watery sign with Rahu and Mars and aspected by Saturn.

6.   When Moon also joins the combination 5, then it gives worst type of tuberculosis.

7.   Mars and Saturn aspect a watery sign in lagna.

8.   Sun and Moon exchange sign in birth chart or in Navamsha and any one is aspected by malefic.

9.   Sun and Moon together in cancer or Leo and aspected by malefic.

10.   Saturn and Moon together and aspected by Mars.

11.   Sun, Jupiter and Saturn in fourth house.

12.   Fourth house afflicted and a malefic in sixth or eighth house.

13.   Mars in Cancer, Sun in Libra and Saturn in Capricorn.

14.   Lagna lord and Venus conjoined in a trik house.

15.   Lagna aspected by Mars and Saturn.

16.   Mercury in cancer. In our view this Mercury should be under malefic influence.

Heart

Moon is the significator of heart and Sun is the significator of heart disease. Fourth house is the seat of heart. The signs Taurus, Cancer and Pisces rule the circulation of blood. Mars is blood. Saturn is the cause of palpitation and Ketu is the giver of pain.

1.   Mars and Ketu in fourth house.

2.   Moon in malefic sign and is afflicted.

3.   Sun and Saturn in trik house.

4.   Sun and lord of sixth house placed in fourth house with a malefic.

5.   Moon is afflicted in fourth house and malefic in trik house.

6.   Sun as sixth lord is placed in fourth house with a malefic.

7.   Saturn or Jupiter is the sixth lord and is placed in fourth house and is aspected by malefic.

8.   Mars, Saturn and Jupiter are in third house associated with malefic.

Breast

Moon is the significator of breast and fourth house is the seat. Fourth house is right and tenth house is left breast. Mars is the significator of glands of breast and Venus is the giver of breast disease. All earthy signs govern the flesh of body.

1.   When Moon and fourth house are afflicted, this disease is caused.

2.   When sixth lord makes a relation with fourth house.

Spleen

Jupiter is the significator and fifth house contains spleen. Mars and Ketu cause tumors. Moon and Mars control the blood.

1.   Malefic Jupiter is in lagna or in trik house.

2.   Mars in lagna and sixth lord is weak and afflicted.

3.   Moon in papa kartari and Saturn in seventh house.

4.   Waning Moon in a sign of Saturn in lagna and Saturn in sixth or eighth house.

Liver

Jupiter is the significator of liver and fifth house is the seat. Sun and Mars control the bile and Moon controls blood.

1.   Lagna lord and Jupiter occupy sixth or eighth house.

2.   Mars and Moon in sixth house cause jaundice.

3.   Moon as sixth lord is aspected by malefic gives jaundice.

4.   Moon is lord of lagna or seventh house and is aspected by malefic only.

5.   Saturn in lagna also gives jaundice.

Diabetes

1.   Combust Jupiter in Rahu Ketu axis.

2.   Saturn and Rahu afflict Jupiter.

3.   Venus in sixth house and Jupiter in twelfth house.

4.   Jupiter debilitated or placed in trik house. Any malefic relation with such Jupiter will aggravate the disease.

5.   Lord of fifth house is in conjunction with any trik lord.

6.   Jupiter retrograde is afflicted in trik house. The disease is present when Jupiter is in any house other than a trik house.

Gall Bladder

1.   Mercury is conjoined with lagna lord and sixth lord.

2.   Sun is with a malefic and aspected by a malefic.

3.   Sun in eighth house and a malefic in second house and Mars is weak.

4.   Moon in the sign of Mars and is in papa kartari.

5.   Lord of sixth house is in eighth house with Sun and a malefic.

6.   Saturn, Mars and Jupiter together in lagna.

7.   Sixth lord is with Venus, Mars and Saturn.

8.   Mars in Cancer and Sun in Capricorn.

9.   Venus, Sun and Saturn conjoined.

10.   Sun or Mars in eighth house and a malefic in second
       house.

11.   Rahu in eighth house and aspected by a malefic.

12.   Mercury and sixth lord in lagna.

Limbs

Defective limb

1.   Saturn is in seventh house and Mars is with Rahu or is
      weak.

2.   Malefic in Aries, Cancer, Scorpio, Capricorn and Pisces
      and Moon and Saturn occupy ninth house then person
      is lame.

3.   Saturn placed in sixth house gives problems in feet and
      back.

4.   Venus is in lagna and aspected by Saturn then there is
      short coming in waist.

5.   The lords of eighth and ninth house is placed in fourth
      from a malefic and are with a malefic and also aspected
      by a malefic then there is short coming in thighs.

6.   Rahu, Mars and Saturn in sixth house makes a person
      lame.

7.   Sun, Mars and Saturn in sixth house make a person
      lame.

8.   Sun, Moon and Saturn in sixth or in eighth house give
      troubles of hands.

9.   Venus is placed in fourth house. Saturn or Mercury or
      Mars is in association of Jupiter in any house, there
      will be defect in hands, back or feet.

10.   Afflicted Saturn and Moon are placed in fifth or ninth
       house.

Loss of limb

1.   Moon in tenth house, Mars in seventh house and Sun in second house.

2.   Mars occupy lagna in Drekkana and aspected by Saturn, Sun and Moon then the head is not there.

3.   When Mars occupy fifth house in the above combination then arms are not there.

4.   When Mars occupy ninth house in the above combination then legs are not there.

5.   Saturn and sixth lord in twelfth house and aspected by a malefic cause loss of thigh.

6.   Saturn, Mars, Mercury and Jupiter are conjoined and Venus is in fourth house in a day birth, the person is without forearm.

7.   Saturn and Venus are in sixth house then also no forearm.

8.   Saturn is placed in seventh house with Rahu or Mars and is weak.

9.   Mars occupy fifth or ninth house and is aspected by malefic.

Hydrocele

1.   Venus and Mars together in eighth house.

2.   Venus in the sign of Mars and associated with Mars.

3.   Venus and Moon in the sign of Mars and aspected by Jupiter and Saturn.

Impotency

1.   When a male sign rises in birth chart and in Navamsha chart.

2.   Venus and Moon occupy male sign in birth and Navamsha chart.

3.   Venus and Saturn in tenth house.

4.   Saturn is in sixth or 12th house from Venus.

Foul smell from body

1.   Venus in the sign of Saturn.

2.   Lord of sixth house in Gemini, Virgo or Capricorn.

3.   Venus and Mercury conjoined in an angular house in a sign of Mercury.

4.   Saturn and Venus are in their sign in Trimshamsha.

5.   Moon in lagna in Aries.

Skin disease

1.   Lagna lord, eighth lord and Saturn or Rahu or Ketu are together in sixth house the disease develops in the dasha of lagna lord or eighth lord.

2.   When lagna lord and Sun are in a trik house the person gets boils on skin.

3.   Mars and Saturn in sixth or in eleventh house give boils on skin.

Leprosy

1.   Moon, Mars and Saturn in Aries or Taurus.

2.   Venus, Mars, Saturn and Moon in Cancer, Scorpio or Pisces.

3.   Malefic in Cancer, Scorpio and Pisces.

4.   Moon in tenth house, Mercury in Aries and Mars and Saturn conjunct in any house.

5.   Moon, Mars, Venus and Saturn are in watery signs, singly or jointly, and afflicted by malefic.

6.   Moon occupies Navamsha of Gemini or Cancer or Pisces and aspected by Mars and Saturn.

7.   Any of the signs Taurus or Cancer or Scorpio or Capricorn fall in trine and is afflicted by malefic.

8.   Moon, Mercury and lagna lord are in Rahu Ketu axis.

9.   Saturn or Sun is in lagna with sixth lord.

10.   Mars in lagna, Sun in eighth house and Saturn in fourth house.

11.   Afflicted Moon and Venus are in watery signs.

12.   Moon in lagna, Sun in seventh, Saturn and Mars placed in second or twelfth house.

13.   Jupiter in sixth house, Moon is in the sign of Jupiter. (19th or 22nd year)

14.   Moon and Saturn in sixth house gives blood leprosy.

15.   Mars or Mercury is the lagna lord and is conjunct Moon or Rahu or Saturn.

16.   Lagna lord is not placed in lagna. Moon and Rahu in lagna gives white leprosy. Mars and Rahu in lagna give red leprosy. Saturn and Rahu give black leprosy.

Ring worm

1.   Moon in second house in a movable and watery sign.

2.   Moon with Saturn or Sun is placed in lagna.

Impotency

1.   Both Sun and full Moon are in odd sign.

2.   Mercury and Saturn are in odd signs and aspect each other.

3.   Mars placed in odd sign and aspects Sun in even sign.

4.   Mars placed in odd sign and aspects lagna and Moon placed in odd sign.

5.   Mercury is in odd sign and Moon in even sign and both are aspected by Mars.

6.   Lagna, Moon and Mercury are in odd sign and odd Navamsha and are aspected by Saturn and Venus.

7.   Mars is in seventh house and aspected by malefic. (This also give urinary problems)

8.   Certain placements of planets in odd or even signs induce impotency.

Even Sign	Odd Sign
Moon	Sun
Saturn	Mercury
Sun	Mars
Moon	Mars
Lagna	Mars
Moon	Mercury

9.   Moon, lagna and Venus occupy odd Navamsha.

10.   Saturn and Venus in tenth or eighth house.

11.   Saturn is in sixth or twelfth house from Venus.

12.   Saturn is in sixth or twelfth house and is debilitated.

Mental Malady

1.   Sun in lagna, Moon in twelfth and Mars is in a trine.

2.   Moon, Saturn and Gulika occupy Kendra.

3.   Moon and Saturn are in Kendra and not aspected by benefic.

4.   Sun in lagna, Moon in a trine and Jupiter is in third house.

5.   Sun and Gulika are in second house and aspected by two malefic or Saturn is with third lord.

6.   Saturn in fifth house and aspects lagna lord and fifth lord is with a malefic.

Secret illness

1. Moon in cancer or Scorpio and associated with malefic.

2. Mercury and sixth lord with Mars.

3. A malefic in eighth house.

4. Jupiter in twelfth house.

Blood disease

1. Mars is in first, sixth, seventh or twelfth house.

2. Mars is conjoined with Gulika.

3. Mars is aspected by Sun.

4. Mars is eclipsed.

5. Mars is in enemy sign or is debilitated.

6. Mars is in second or eighth house with Gulika and second lord is also related to Gulika.

UPGRAHA

The role of Upgraha is important. The placement of these is seen in the chart.

1. Dhoom placed in second house makes a person devoid of a limb.

2. Dhoom placed in sixth house will give disease free life.

3. Vyatipat placed in sixth house makes a person physically strong.

4. Vyatipat placed in eighth house gives disorders of blood and deformed eyes.

5. Vyatipat in twelfth house makes a person disabled.

6. Placement of Paridhi in eighth house gives strong body.

7. Paridhi in eleventh house gives poor digestion.

8. Indrachap in third house then the person is without a limb.

9.   Indrachap in fourth house will give immunity from disease.

10. Indrachap in eleventh house also give freedom from disease.

11. Upketu placed in third house gives thin body and severe disease.

12. Gulika in lagna gives suffering from disease.

13. Gulika in fourth house gives sickly body and windy, bilious disorders.

14. Gulika in sixth house gives strong limbs.

15. Gulika in twelfth house gives some handicap.

Chapter 7

Locate Disease

We give a step-by-step approach to locate the disease and to assess the nature of disease. Beside the basic birth chart, we will use the following divisional charts to understand the disease.

1. Saptvimshamsha.

2. Drekkana

3. Shodashamsha

Parashar has declared "भांशे चैव बलाबलम्" meaning that D 27 indicates the strength and weakness of a person.

The most important and useful chart to locate disease is D 27. Parashar has given this chart to see the strength of a person. So we can assess the strength and weakness of a person from this divisional chart. This is the main research of the author. It is actually given by Parashar but not interpreted in this context. Most of astrologers simply ignore this chart.

Step 1

Prepare Saptvimshamsha chart along with the longitudes of planets in this chart. Method of working the longitude is given in the divisional chart chapter.

Step 2

Analyze this chart for strength of a person. Standard approach is given. These are golden rules and never to be ignored.

1.   Check the lagna of D 27. A strong lagna is a must for healthy body.

2.   Mars is the indicator of physical strength. A strong Mars assures good physical strength.

3.   Strength of Moon gives healthy mind.

4.   Now see the afflicted planets and **signs**. The affliction is caused by Malefic including Rahu and Ketu. Affliction by Ketu gives mysterious problems.

5.   The afflicted planet and sign is the disease. The sign and Nakshatra occupied by the planet in D 27 indicate the area of disease.

6.   The sense indicated by afflicted planet is harmed. For example, if Venus is afflicted than vision or eye sight is the problem. Jupiter is the cause of hearing loss. Mercury gives speech problems.

7.   The planets causing affliction are the promoters of disease.

8.   More afflictions to the same planet give serious problems.

9.   Diseases of long duration like cancer etc. are caused by Saturn and or Rahu.

10. Mars and Ketu indicate surgery. Saturn indicates removal of body part.

11. The eighth lord of D 1 along with eighth lord of D 27 is also a cause of disease. If it is related to lagna/ lagna lord of D 27 then it causes congenital disease. The dasha at birth is most important. If the dasha at birth is related to eighth house/ lord then it is a confirmation of congenital disease.

12. Affliction by Rahu indicates infection and promotes the disease to uncontrollable levels. It also gives illness due to wrong medication which acts as poison.

13.   The cure or continuation of disease is decided by the dasha.

14.   Healthy chart

   a.   Lagna is having relation with Benefics (But are not the lords of trik houses).

   b.   Mars, Sun and Jupiter are strong and related with Benefics.

   c.   To check the capacity to cure and fight disease is seen from the relation of trine lords. The trine lords of birth chart or D 27 should have mutual connection in D 27.

15.   Multiple diseases

   a.   Sun is debilitated and associated with Malefic. It takes away the strength to fight the disease.

   b.   Lagna and lagna lord are weak and afflicted.

   c.   Mars is not related to a friendly sign rising in lagna.

Step 3

Drekkana is used to see the seat of ailment. This is used to decide whether the disease is of internal or external side of the part of body. This has been discussed in the divisional chart chapter. Any planet in first half of a Drekkana gives internal disease and in second half gives external disease. This is seen in D27. The longitude of concerned planet is seen in D 27. If longitude is in first half part of Drekkana then disease is internal. When in second part of Drekkana then it is external.

Step 4

The cause of disease is the afflicting planet. The Tridosha of this cause is now examined. For example, if the cause is Saturn, then the cause is Vaat or the dryness. Jupiter is fat and so on. Disease caused by Ketu is not easily diagnosed.

The Tridosha have been explained in the earlier chapters. The afflicted planet or sign is the seat of disease. It is also the disease.

Step 5

Now comes the timing of disease. It is the dasha of the afflicted planet which generally triggers the disease. The onset of disease is the dasha of afflicting planet. We can ascertain the time of onset of disease and take precautions. Dasha is seen in D1 as per the standard approach of analyzing Vimshottary dasha. D 27 is also suitable to analyze dasha for diseases.

The timing can be confirmed from D 16. It is the chart which shows happiness or sorrow. A well placed and well-connected planet gives happiness. Reverse gives disease.

The timing of cure or recovery can be ascertained by the following approach. These are applied in D1.

a.   Note the dasha at the time of onset of disease. The twelfth house from dasha gives cure. These can be from PD, AD or MD.

b.   The dasha of planets or lords of trine can give relief.

c.   In D 16 the angles give happiness. Planets in angles or the lords of angles when not connected with trik lords give happiness in their dasha.

d.   In this way we should check the next dasas.

We will now illustrate the method with few examples. These examples are given to illustrate the application of the method.

Example1. Accident. DOB 6 August 1972, TOB 04.25 POB Krasnodar Russia

This chart is given to highlight the importance of sign in D 27.

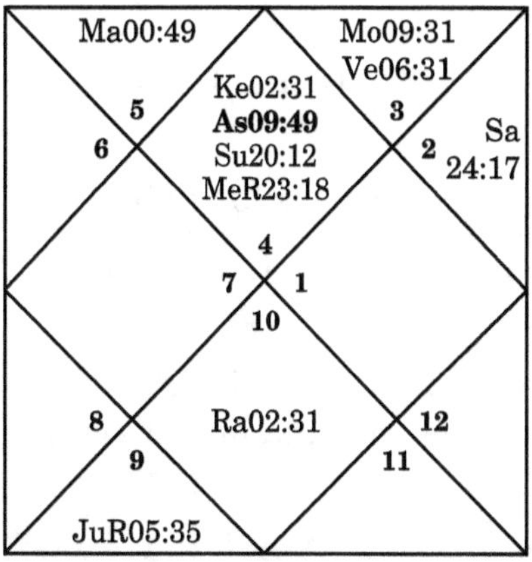

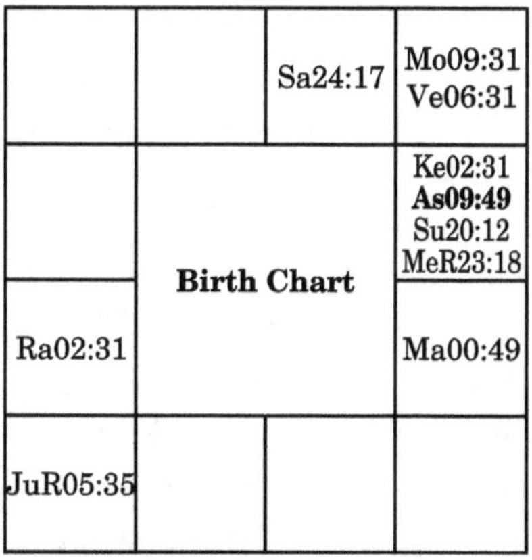

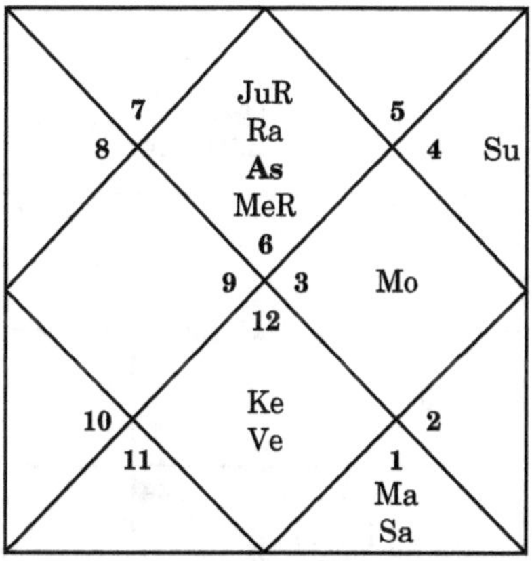

She met with a serious car accident on 15 December 2015. She suffered head, hand and leg injury. The Vimshottary dasha running was Saturn/ Mars. Mars is lord of eighth house in D 27. The signs under malefic influence are;

1.	Aries. Aries is head of kaal Purush. It is occupied by sixth and eighth lord. Association of house lord or benefic with trik houses makes them strong. There is no benefic aspect.

2.   Gemini. Saturn aspects it. Moon is placed in Gemini and indicates Chest problems in relation to significations of Moon and Gemini.

3.   Cancer. Mars is aspecting Sun and Cancer. Sun is heart and bones.

4.   Libra. Mars and Saturn aspects Libra. Libra is the area of lower abdomen.

5.   Scorpio. Mars is aspecting it. Scorpio is lower back.

6.   Capricorn. Saturn and Sun aspects it. Capricorn is knee and knee joints.

The Antar dasha lord Mars is at 22 degrees in D 27. It is first half of third Drekkana and gives internal injury. Saturn gives external injury.

Example, Saddam Hussein. DOB 28 April 1951, TOB 08.11.45, POB Tikrit

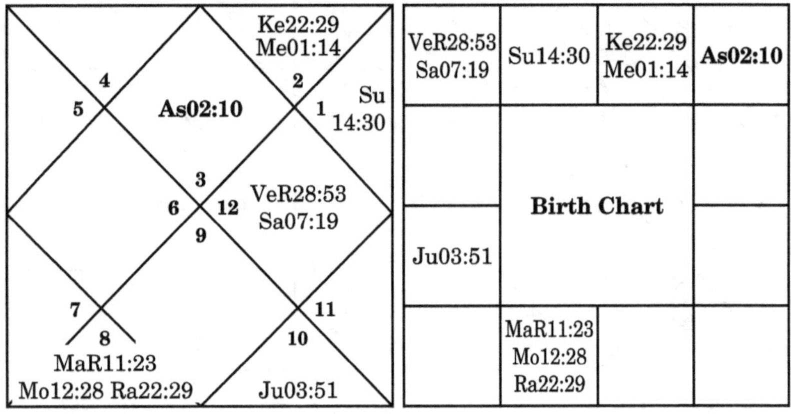

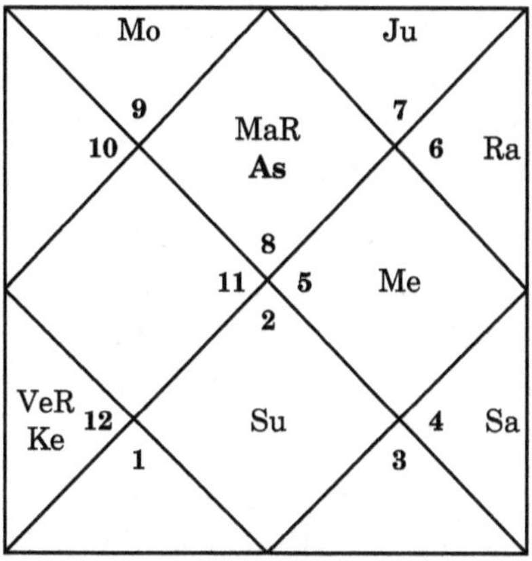

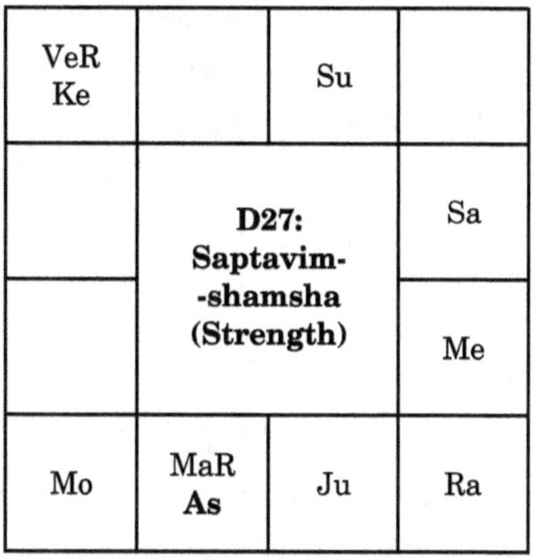

Left chart (D1): Mo (9, house 10) · Ju (7) · MaR As (8) · Ra (6) · Me (5, 2) · 11 · VeR Ke (12, 1) · Su · Sa (4, 3)

Right chart — D27: Saptavim-shamsha (Strength): VeR Ke | | Su | ; | D27 | Sa ; | | | Me ; Mo | MaR As | Ju | Ra

This chart is taken to show sound health. The birth chart is first seen for the sound health.

D 1 Lagna is aspected by sixth lord Mars. Lagna lord Mercury is with Ketu and is aspected by Mars and Saturn. This is not promising good health. This is deceptive as he was in good health. Health is seen from Saptvimshamsha.

D 27 Lagna rising is Scorpio. Lord of lagna Mars is in lagna. Lagna is in Subh kartari. Promise of good health is confirmed.

No one can have a perfect chart. In D 27 Venus is afflicted by Ketu and have no benefic connection. We expect problems governed by Venus. Association of Ketu gives mysterious disease. Another planet in papa kartari is Mercury. Mercury is in Leo sign and Magha Nakshatra. Mercury is eighth lord also. Venus is in U. Bhadrapad. Venus gives diabetes and Kidney problems. He was under Kidney treatment and was undergoing dialysis. Venus is in Pisces and the disease is showing in feet. Mercury gives skin problems. Third planet is Sun. It is aspected by Mars. Sun under influence of Mars give hypertension and bone problems. Mercury is in Leo and with afflicted Sun it points to heart problem.

D 3 The side and cause of diseased part is seen from D 3. Venus is in second part of Drekkana and denotes external cause creating disease. Mercury is in first part and the cause is internal. Sun is in second part and cause is external.

Tatva The afflicted planet is the Tridosha which suffers due to the Tatva of afflicting planet. Venus is watery and stands for phlegmatic and windy dosha. Ketu is causing affliction. Ketu is also phlegmatic and windy. This is the problem in kidney. Mercury is all three humors.

Timing Venus is the afflicted planet. The diseases given by Venus will come in its dasha. Venus operated from 1967 to 1987. Ketu is the afflicting planet and its dasha from 1960 is the onset of this disease. Venus period is giver of disease as it is afflicted.

Example Cancer DOB 23 December 1965, TOB 04.15, POB Mumbai

South Indian chart (Birth Chart):

		Ra11:13	JuR02:14
Sa18:24		**Birth Chart**	
Ma06:23 Ve16:56			
Su07:31 Mo08:19	Ke11:13 Me15:49	As27:57	

North Indian chart:

- House 8: Ke11:13, Me15:49, Su07:31, Mo08:19
- Ascendant: As27:57
- Ma06:23, Ve16:56
- Sa18:24
- JuR02:14
- Ra11:13

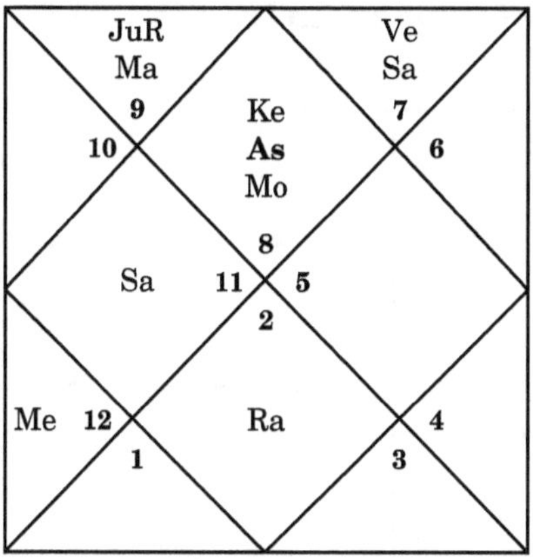

<table>
<tr><td colspan="2">JuR Ma
9
10</td><td colspan="2">Ke
As
Mo
8</td><td colspan="2">Ve Sa
7
6</td></tr>
<tr><td colspan="2">Sa</td><td>11</td><td>5
2</td><td colspan="2"></td></tr>
<tr><td colspan="2">Me 12
1</td><td colspan="2">Ra</td><td colspan="2">4
3</td></tr>
</table>

Me		Ra	
Sa	**D27: Saptavim- -shamsha (Strength)**		
JuR Ma	Ke **As** Mo	Ve Sa	

This person suffered from cancer of intestine. He was operated in July 2005 in Mars Rahu.

D 1 Lagna is aspected by retrograde sixth lord Jupiter. Second house and Mercury are badly afflicted. From this chart the second house problems should be there.

D 27 Moon is with Ketu and aspected by Saturn. This is the combination of cancer. Moon is in Scorpio and governs water and emotions. Scorpio represents intestines. The longitude of Moon in D 27 is 14 deg. 36 min. The micro-Nakshatra is Jyeshtha. Jyeshtha governs colon bowels and anus.

D3 Moon is in second part of Drekkana and cause of disease is external.

Tatva Moon is water. The watery element is vitiated by Saturn which is airy and cause dryness. The disease was caused by contaminated water.

Timing Moon dasha was from 1994 to 2004 and the disease spread during this period. He was operated in 2005.

Example K N Rao DOB 13 October 1931, TOB 07.53, POB Machilipatnam

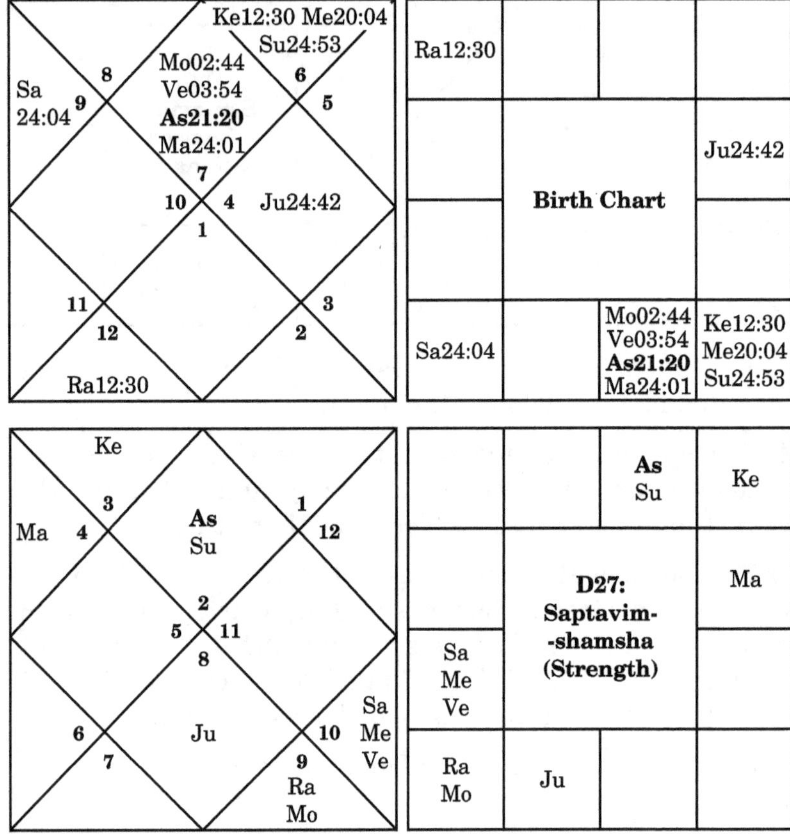

D 1 Lagna lord is in lagna and assures good health. Sixth lord Jupiter is exalted in tenth house. A strong lord promotes the significations of the house. Disease is a signification of sixth house and Jupiter will promote it.

D 27 Lagna is with Sun and aspected by eighth lord Jupiter. Mars is debilitated but with cancellation. Planets afflicted are Venus, Mercury, Moon and Jupiter. The diseases are given by them. Jupiter and Venus give diabetics and kidney liver problems. Moon gives problem to left eye. Venus and Moon both are significator of eye sight. Mercury and Venus in Capricorn give problems in legs. Their association with Saturn and aspect of Mars create paralytic condition of legs.

D 3 Mercury is in first part of Drekkana and gives internal disease in legs. Moon is in first part and eye disease is internal. Venus is also in first part.

Tatva Mercury represents all three Tatva. It is afflicted by Saturn creating dryness. Association with afflicted Venus causes inability to assimilate water. Moon is watery and trouble is by Rahu. Rahu is windy and the suffering is from air.

Timing Mercury Saturn operated in 2001 to 2003. Problems were felt in legs and he was not able to walk. When this dasha ended the problem also ended. Moon is afflicted by Rahu Ketu axis. In Ketu Moon the eye problem surfaced and was cured by surgery.

In D 16 Mercury is in eighth house and aspected by Mars. Mercury does not give happiness.

Example Deaf & Dumb DOB 30 November 2000, TOB 12.05, POB Rewari

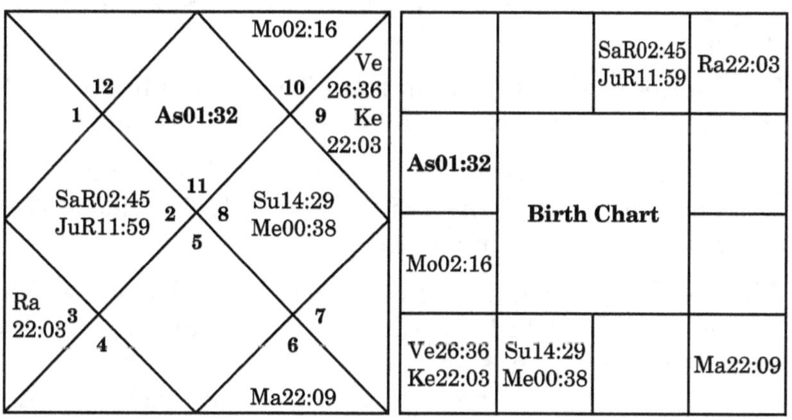

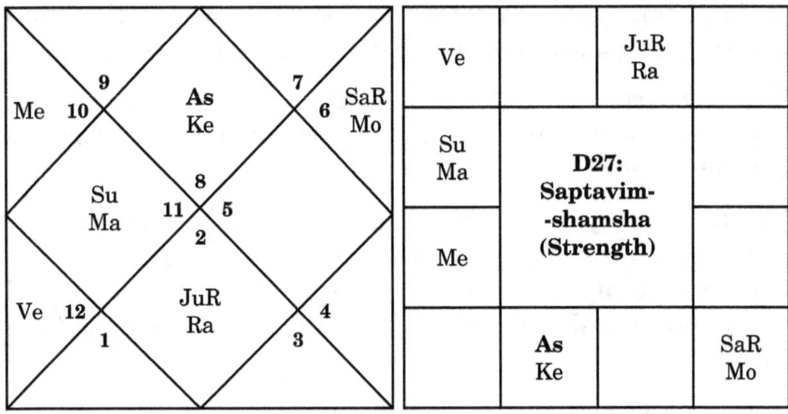

D 1 Second house and lord are under malefic influence. Problem to second house and significator of speech is seen. Second house and Jupiter signify many other factors. From D 1 we cannot say for sure about any one factor. This is to be confirmed from another divisional chart.

D27 Jupiter is under double affliction by Rahu and Mars. Here also Jupiter is second lord. The natural physical signification of Jupiter is speech. The sign afflicted is Taurus and speech is afflicted. Jupiter governs larynx and vocal cords.

D 3 Jupiter is at 23 d- 40m in D 27. This falls in first part of Drekkana. In first part the problem is due to internal cause.

Tatva Jupiter is ether and is the void. He is under affliction by Mars and Rahu. Mars is fiery and Rahu is windy. The cause is heat and air unbalance.

Timing The problem started in Moon dasha. Moon is sixth lord of birth chart. In D 27 it is with Saturn and is placed in Virgo which is eighth sign of birth. The dasha to follow are Mars, Rahu, Jupiter and Saturn. All are involved in giving disease and no respite is seen.

Example birth defect DOB 1 January 1983, TOB 07.22, POB Red Bank, NJ, USA

This chart is taken from astro data bank. He was born with congenital heart disease. He required open heart surgery within twelve hours of birth.

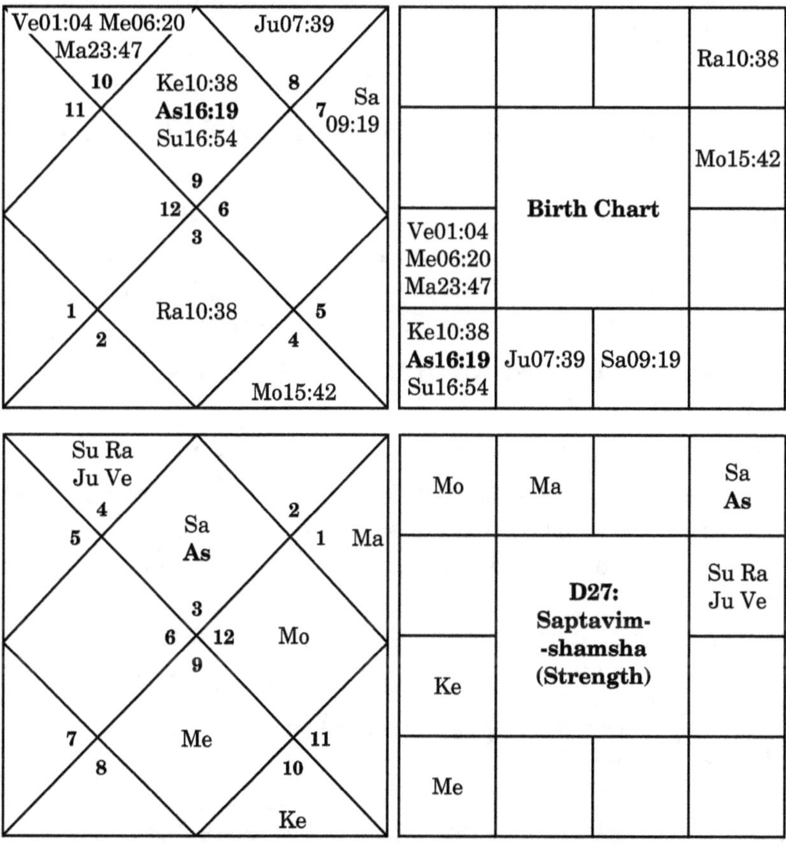

D1 Lagna is occupied by Ketu and ninth lord Sun. It is aspected by exalted Saturn. Dasha at birth was Saturn/ Jupiter/ Ketu. It is not pointing to birth defect. The karaka of first house is Sun. Sun is with Ketu and aspected by Saturn. Double affliction to Sun indicates body defect. It can be heart disease.

D 27 This gives a clear picture. Lagna is occupied by eighth lord Saturn. The dasha at birth is also of Saturn. The congenital disease is confirmed. Sun is with Rahu and aspected by sixth lord Mars indicating surgery. Mars is trishadaya lord. The sign involved is Cancer. Cancer governs heart. Sun also indicates heart. Association of two Benefics is a saving factor.

D 3 Sun is at 6 degrees in D 27. It indicates external disease.

Tatva The affliction is caused by Rahu and Mars. Rahu is windy and Mars is bilious.

Timing The dasha at birth is of Saturn. Saturn is eighth lord and the problem started in this dasha itself. The next dasha is of Mercury. Mercury is Kendra lord in birth chart and again lagna lord in D 27. It can give relief.

Example Kidney by birth DOB 19 April 1987, TOB 5.38 AM, POB Delhi

This boy was having kidney trouble by birth. He had undergone four operations within four years of birth. First operation was performed on 40th day of birth and fourth on the day he completed four years. This happened in Ketu dasha.

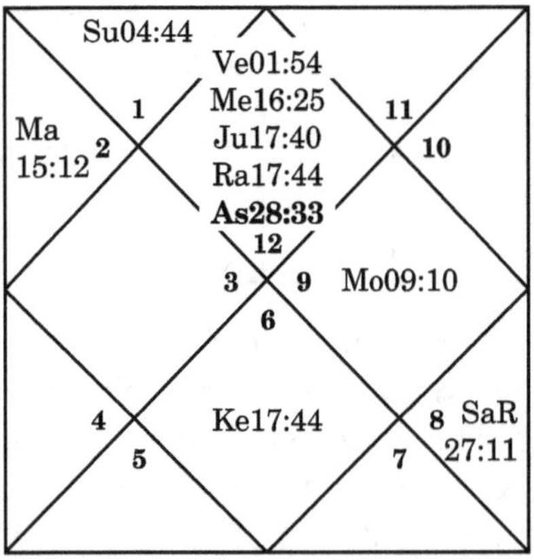

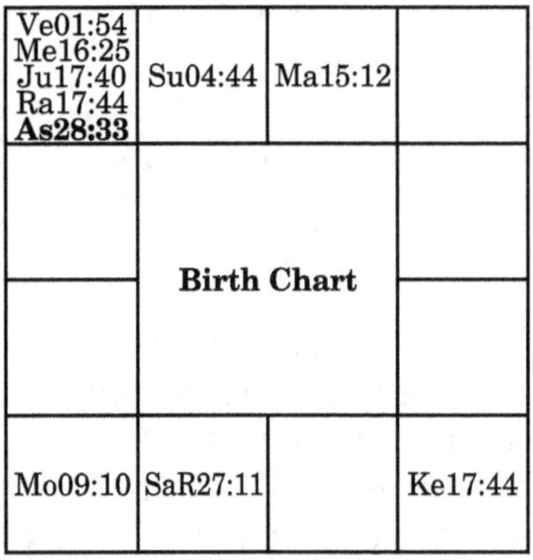

D1 All three Benefics are in lagna including lord of lagna. The seriousness is not seen. Sixth lord is exalted and have no association or aspect. Sixth lord when exalted can give illness unless protected by Benefics.

D 27 Lagna has Venus and is aspected by Mars and Sun. Venus is afflicted and is the disease. Venus governs kidneys along with other significations. Other afflictions are on Mercury and Ketu. Mercury is aspected by Mars and Saturn. Mercury is eighth lord of D 27. Mercury gives disease of skin. Ketu is aspected by Saturn.

D 3 Venus is at 21 degrees in D 27. This is first part of Drekkana and the disease is of internal origin. Mercury is at 23 degrees and indicates internal disease.

Tatva Venus is afflicted by Mars and Sun. Both are bilious and fiery.

Timing Dasha at birth was Ketu/ Mars. In birth chart Ketu is aspected by eighth lord Venus. Venus is in lagna of D 27 and with the dasha of Ketu the disease is by birth.

Venus dasha started on 23 June 1989. On 18 March 2009 in AD of Ketu the stomach dialysis was started but was not successful. The stomach dialysis on 13 April 2009 was successful. The dialysis was continued till 28 May 2009.

Sun dasha started on 23 June 2009. In June 2009 dialysis from throat and hand were tried but failed. The doctors reverted to stomach dialysis from 27 June 2009.

Dasha of Moon is awaited and should be good.

Chapter 8

Examples

Heart

This example is taken from astro databank. It is case number 14842. It is a case of a baby born with congenital heart defect of a missing heart valve. Unsuccessful surgery was done and the child died on 23 January 1983. The dasa was Moon/ Jupiter/ Mars and the Chara dasa was Cancer/ Aquarius.

Example DOB 29 March 1982, TOB 13.01, POB Upland CA USA

Su15:14 Me02:43		Mo14:20	Ra25:04
			As11:57
Ve28:50	Birth Chart		
Ke25:04		JuR15:01	MaR17:21 SaR26:05

North Indian chart (left): As11:57; Ra25:04; Mo14:20; Su15:14, Me02:43; Ve28:50; Ke25:04; JuR15:01; MaR17:21, SaR26:05.

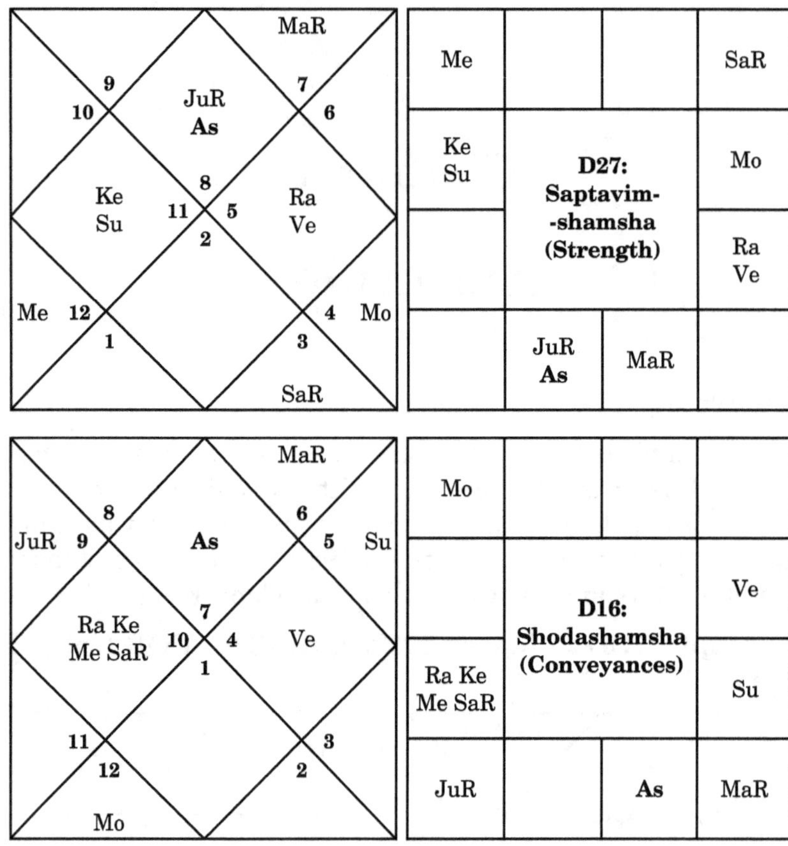

We check D 27. The most afflicted planet is Venus. It is in Rahu Ketu axis and aspected by Sun and Saturn. Saturn is eighth lord of birth and aspects Venus from eighth house of D 27. Venus is the cause of disease. Venus is in Leo which governs heart also. The following observations must be noted in D 27 chart.

1. Lagna rising has retrograde Jupiter who is sixth lord of birth.

2. Lagna lord Mars is in twelfth. Thus, both lagna and lagna lord are weak.

3. Aspect of Saturn on disease causing planet indicates loss of body part. Being eighth lord of birth, it can give chronic disease.

4. The dasha at birth was Moon/ Jupiter/ Saturn. The AD and PD at birth belong to sixth and eighth lord of birth. This gives disease at the time of birth.

5. Venus is in second part of D3 (25 to 30) and in even sign. It indicates internal part.

6. The PD at death was of Saturn. In D16, Saturn is in fourth house and is badly afflicted. It gives loss of comfort. For surgery, we must have the PD of a happiness giver planet. It should not be under the influence of malefic planets in D 16. Saturn is badly afflicted in D 16.

7. The cause of disease is seen from planet afflicting the disease giver. Venus is having affliction from Rahu Ketu, Sun and Saturn. Rahu Ketu is mysterious disease and is not diagnosed easily. Saturn is windy and gives problem due to vaat. It can be dryness. Sun is heat and Pitta.

Example Bill Clinton DOB 19 August 1946 TOB 8.53 POB Hope AR USA

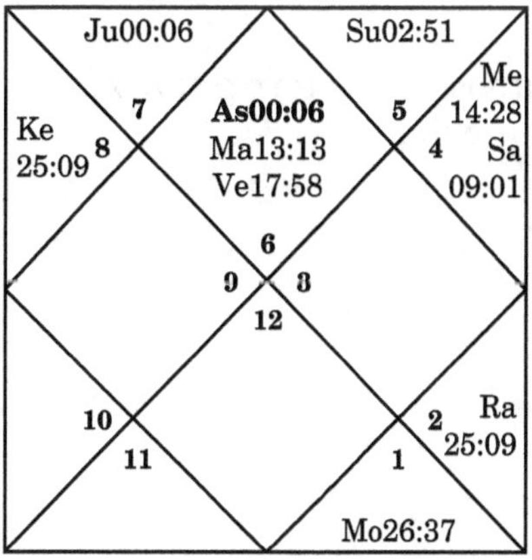

	Mo26:37	Ra25:09	
	Birth Chart		Me14:28 Sa09:01
			Su02:51
	Ke25:09	Ju00:06	**As00:06** Ma13:13 Ve17:58

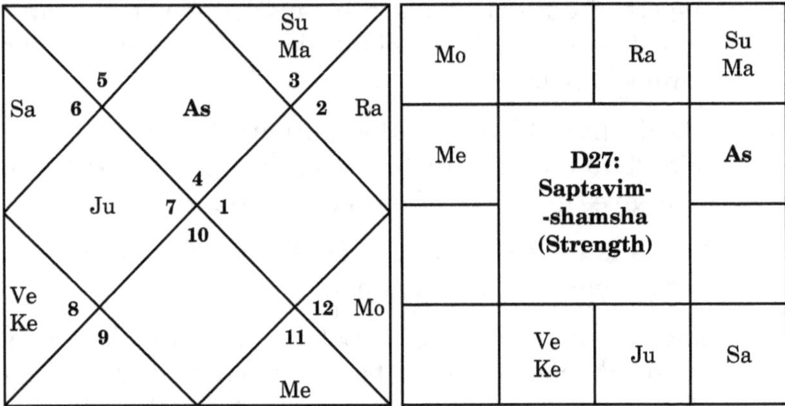

He suffered from heart and lungs diseases. He was operated for heart disease in March 2005 in the dasha of Saturn/ Saturn/ Venus. Lung's operation was done on 11 February 2010. Dasa was Saturn/ Ketu/ Jupiter.

In birth chart, Sun is in own sign Leo. Sun is karaka of heart. The illness is not seen in birth chart. Now we come to D 27. Sun is with Mars and aspected by Saturn. Mars is surgery and Saturn indicates removal and replacement of part. Dasha was of Saturn.

Moon is karaka of lungs. Moon is the other planet afflicted by Saturn. Sign of Gemini is also under heavy affliction. Gemini represent chest.

Sun is at 17 degrees and the problem is internal. Moon is at 29 degrees and is the external problem.

Example DOB 8 September 1949 TOB 23.37 POB Gurdaspur

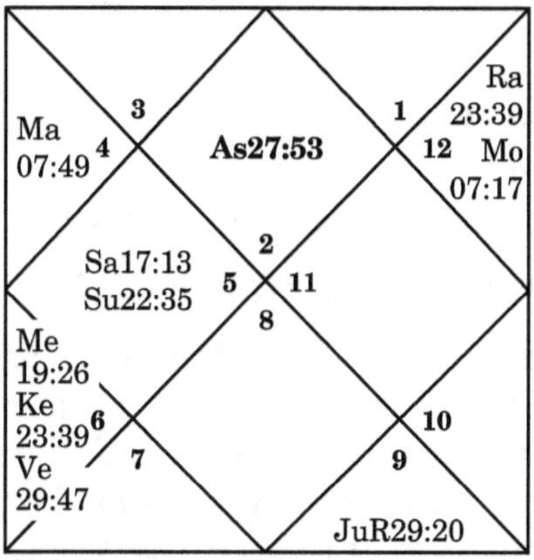

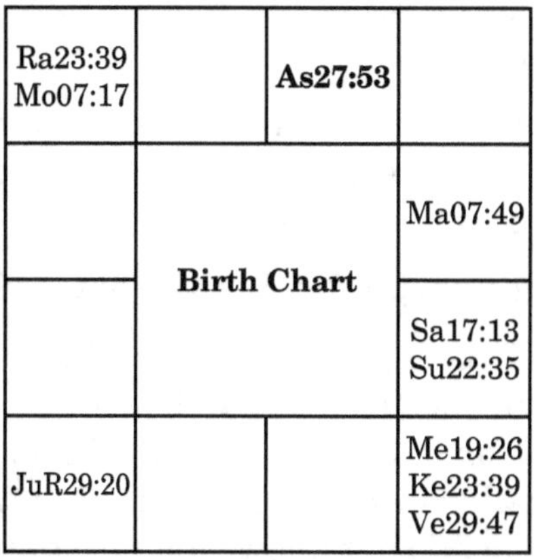

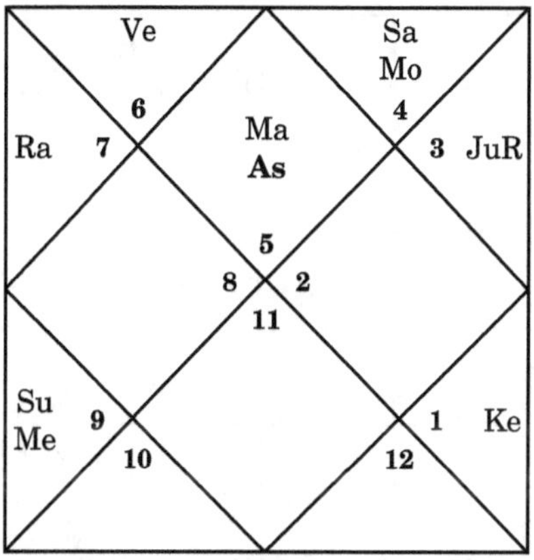

This chart belongs to an athlete who represented India in Olympics in power lifting. First, we examine the physical health of the chart. In D 27, Mars is in lagna. Mars is karaka of physical strength. Lord of lagna is in fifth house with Mercury and aspected by Jupiter. Good physical body is granted.

Now we check the problem areas. In D 27 most afflicted planet is Venus. It is lord of sixth of birth. In D27 it is in papa kartari and aspected by Saturn. Venus occupies Virgo in birth and Saptvimshamsha charts.

He suffered nervous problem in 2002. He is not able to walk, hear or speak after this problem. Saturn rules nerves and is the cause of problem. Dasha running in 2002 was Venus Saturn.

Dasha at birth was Saturn/ Mercury/ Saturn. Saturn and Mercury are not related to eighth house of birth/ Saptvimshamsha charts. It is not a case of congenital disease.

Example DOB 7 October 1974, TOB 17.27, POB Delhi

This chart is of a boy who was in mental delirium. He was physically of sound health but mentally ill. He will jump from roof. Did not eat for many days and roam around in village. When he started eating then he will eat a lot and just do not know when to stop. He died at the age of 28 years.

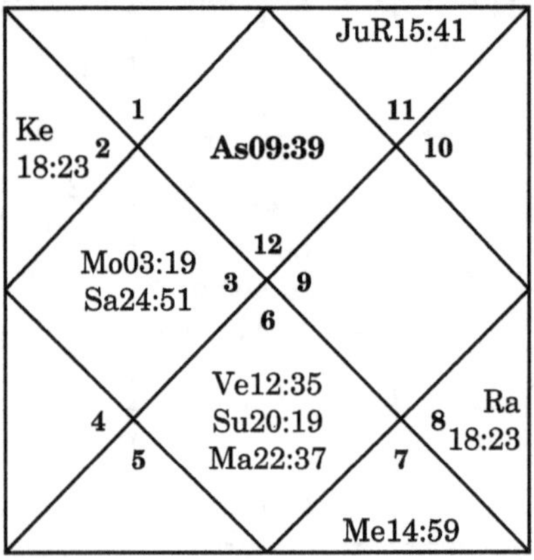

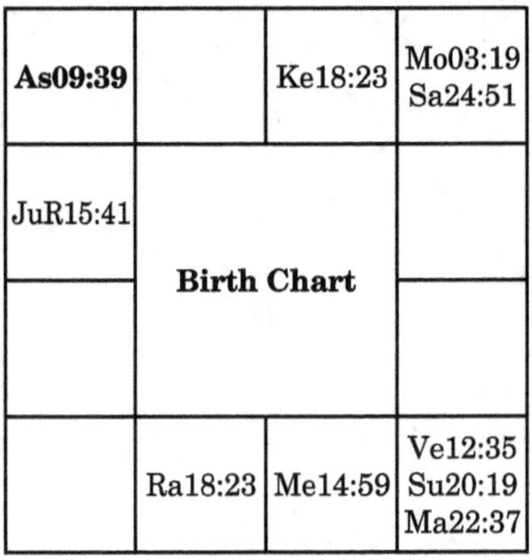

As09:39		Ke18:23	Mo03:19 Sa24:51
JuR15:41	**Birth Chart**		
	Ra18:23	Me14:59	Ve12:35 Su20:19 Ma22:37

South Indian chart (left):
- JuR15:41 (house 11)
- Ke 18:23 (houses 1/2)
- As09:39
- Mo03:19 Sa24:51 (house 3)
- Ve12:35 Su20:19 Ma22:37 (houses 5/6/7)
- Ra 18:23 (house 8)
- Me14:59

In D27 Mars is the eighth lord and aspects lagna. The dasha at birth was of Mars. The illness is from birth. Lord of lagna is with Ketu. Taurus is the most afflicted sign. Its lord is also under the influence of Mars. It gives violence in brain. Venus is eighth lord of birth chart.

Example DOB 6 November 1995, TOB 04.28, POB Alwar

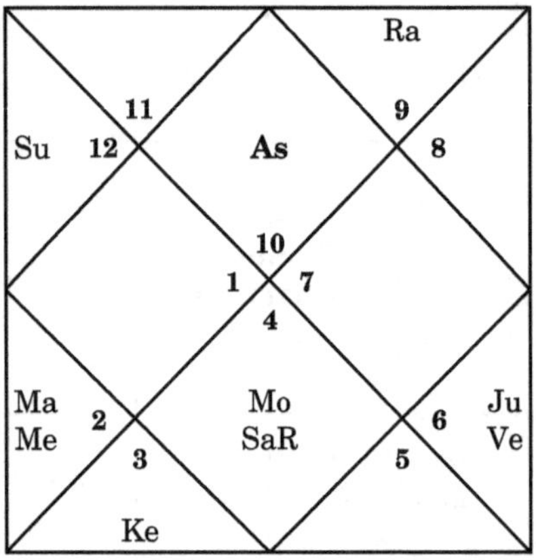

This boy is deaf and dumb. In birth chart second house has affliction. Third house has own lord with two benefics but is unable to speak.

We check D 27. Here Jupiter is third lord and aspected by Saturn and Sun. Jupiter is under affliction and is the cause of dumbness. Dasha at birth was of Ketu. Ketu is in eighth house in D 1. Moon is in eighth house with Ketu and aspected by Sun. This is typical Balarishta and problem is by birth.

Example DOB 4 June 1948, TOB 03.43, POB Srinagar (JK)

Stomach Cancer

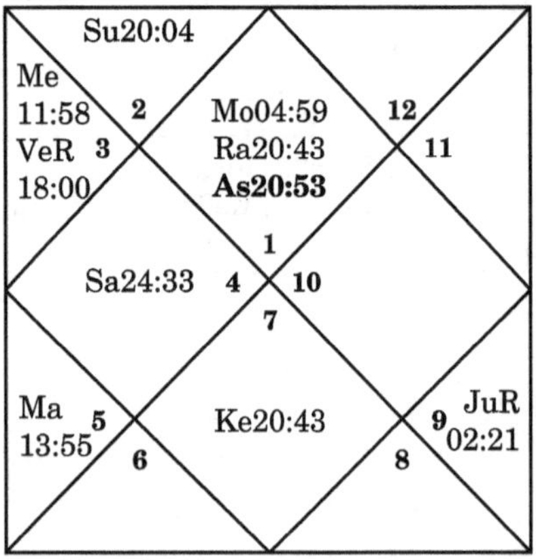

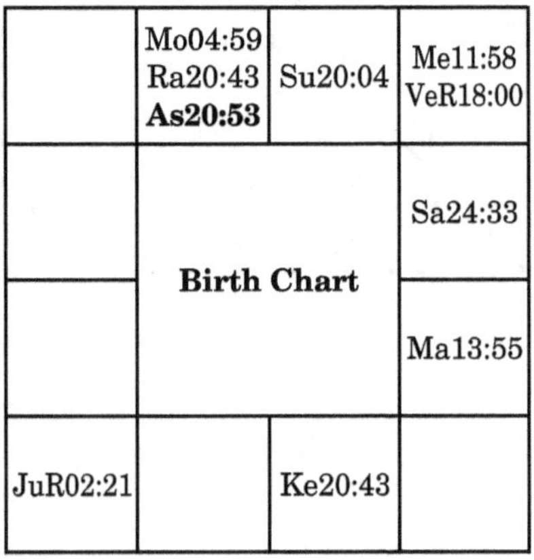

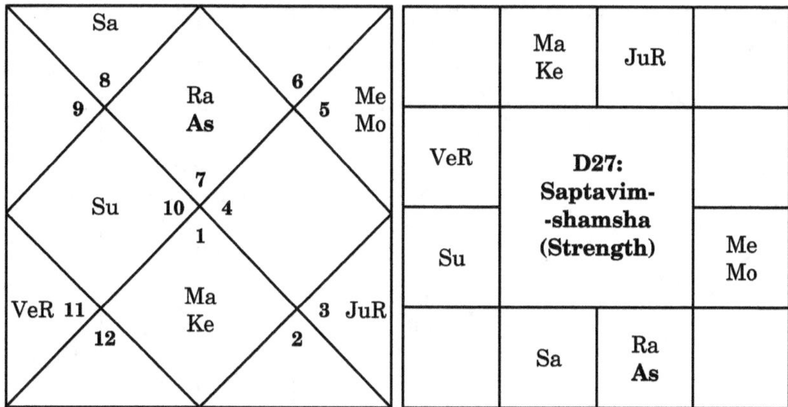

In D 27 Libra is the afflicted sign. Libra contains Rahu and is aspected by Mars and Jupiter. Jupiter is sixth lord as well. Mars is with Ketu. Association of Rahu/ Ketu and Saturn give long term disease like cancer. Surgery was done in June 2004. Dasha was Rahu/ Mercury/Venus. Venus is eighth lord of D 27.

Example. TB. Kamla Nehru DOB 2 August 1899, TOB 01.45.00, POB Delhi

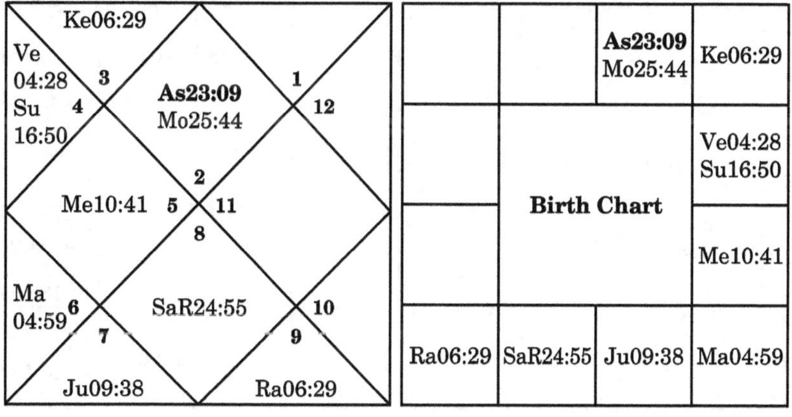

In D 27 Gemini is the afflicted sign. This is fourth house. The fourth lord Mercury is aspected by Saturn. The karaka of fourth house is Moon. Moon is in fourth house. Thus, lagan lord, fourth house, fourth lord and Moon are afflicted. A serious problem is seen in fourth house. She suffered from TB and died in a sanatorium.

Example Asthma DOB 1 September 1923, TOB 22.23.10 POB Meerut

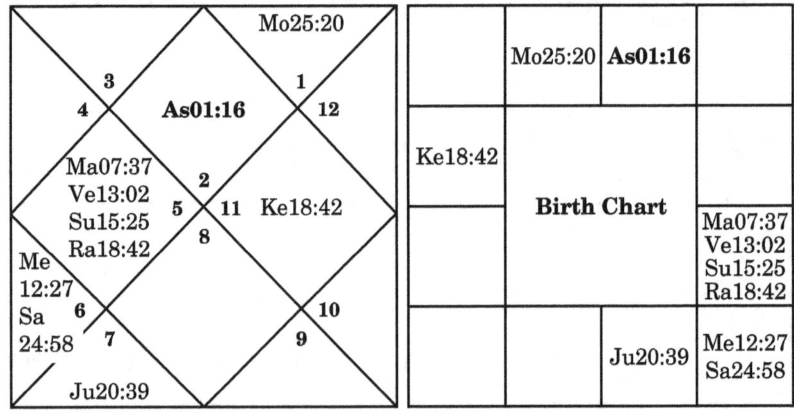

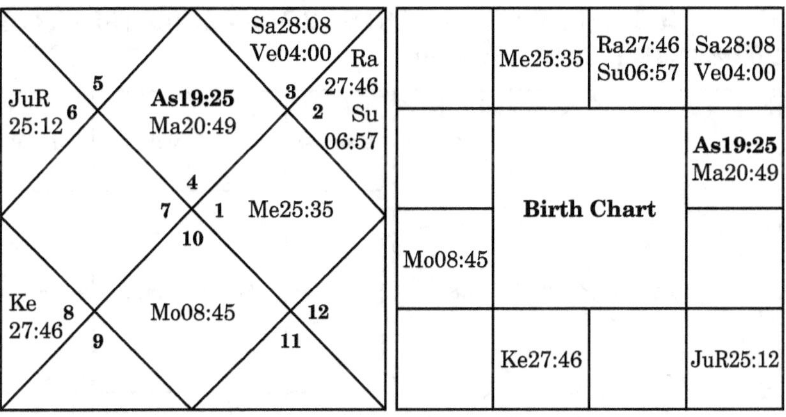

Compare this chart with the chart of Kamla Nehru. In D 27 fourth house and Moon are afflicted. The fourth lord is aspected by eighth lord Jupiter. Here the affliction is by Saturn and give long term disease. In earlier case it was Mars.

Example Polio and legs DOB 21 May 1946, TOB 10.10, POB Los Angeles USA

He suffered from polio at the age of two. Multiple surgeries were performed in 1952, 54, 56. His leg was amputated in 1963.

Moon and Aquarius are under affliction. Aquarius is legs. Mars and Ketu indicate surgery. The dasha at the time of amputation was Mars/ Moon. He was born at the end of Sun dasha. He suffered throughout Moon and Mars dasha.

Example Vaginal Cancer DOB 12 November 1958 TOB 20.08 POB Neuilly France

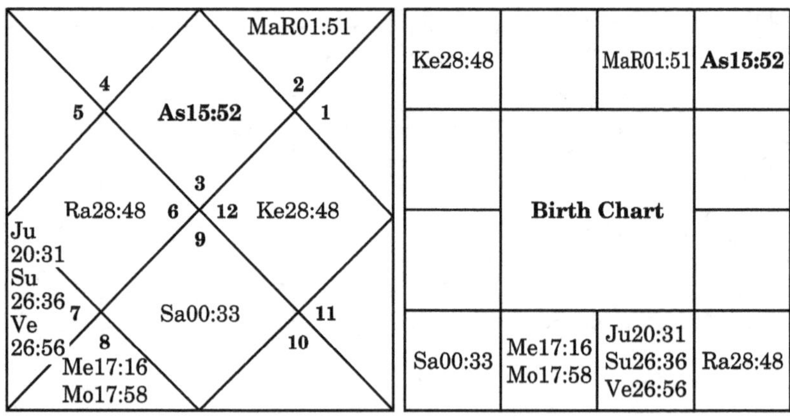

This chart is taken from astro data bank. Case number is 13356. Vaginal cancer was diagnosed in 1975. The dasha was Ketu Venus. In D 27 Venus and Libra are aspected by debilitated Saturn. The Libra sign denotes genitals. Ketu acts as Saturn.

Example Brain clot DOB 11 May 1941 TOB 15.50 POB Delhi

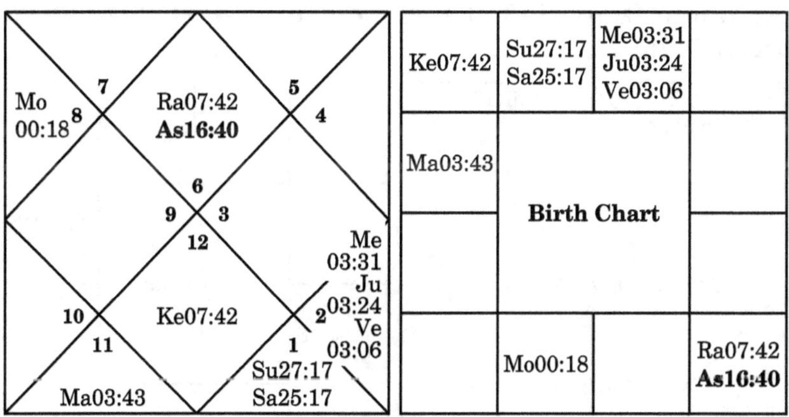

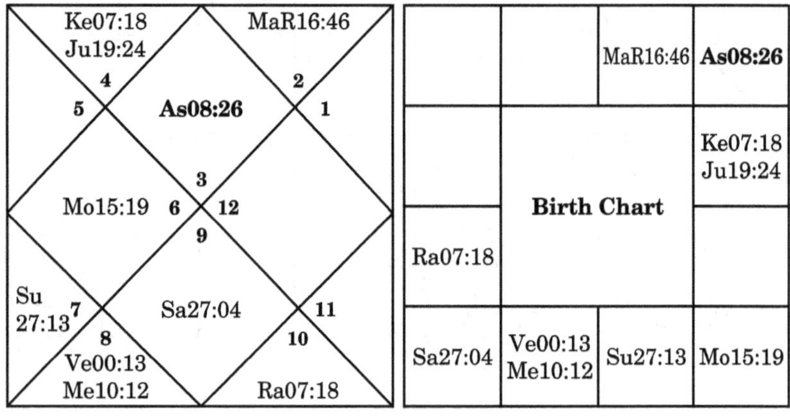

The lagan lord is debilitated in 12th house and has no benefic association or aspect. It shows careless attitude towards health. He suffered from many diseases like diabetes, hypertension and blood clot in brain. He died of brain clot. Aries is aspected by Saturn and Mars. Mars is lord of Aries. Mars is also afflicted by Rahu. Association of Saturn and Rahu gives malignant clot.

Example Diabetic DOB 13 November 1990 TOB 20.06 POB Delhi

This is a case of severe diabetic patient. She suffered from a young age of 13 years. It was start of Rahu dasha. See the condition of Venus in D 27. It is with Rahu and aspected by Mars and Saturn. Venus is in Capricorn and it gives problems in legs. There is danger of imputation of legs.

Example Liz Taylor DOB 23 February 1933 TOB 02.14.10 POB London

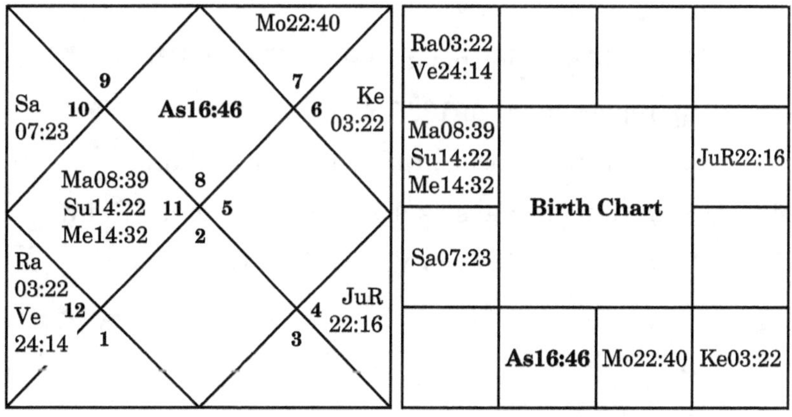

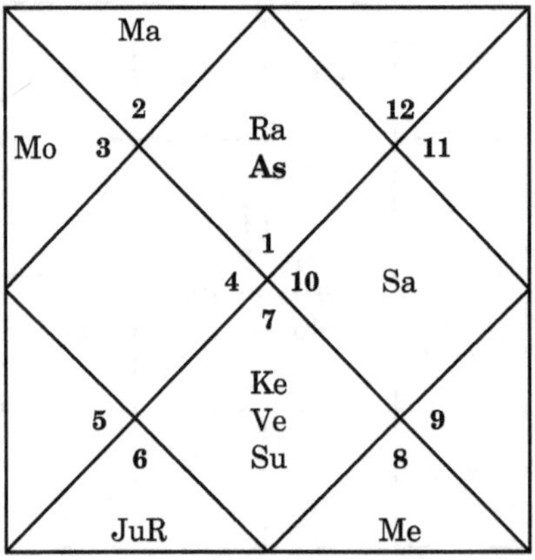

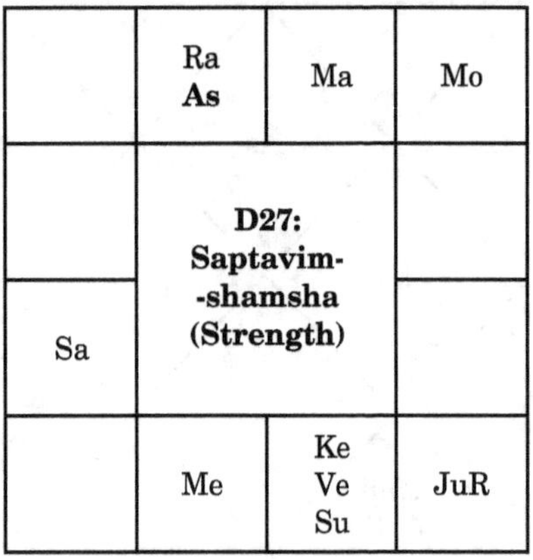

<table>
<tr><td colspan="2">Ma
2</td><td>12</td></tr>
<tr><td>Mo 3</td><td>Ra
As</td><td>11</td></tr>
<tr><td>4</td><td>1
10   Sa
7</td><td></td></tr>
<tr><td>5
6</td><td>Ke
Ve
Su</td><td>9
8</td></tr>
<tr><td>JuR</td><td></td><td>Me</td></tr>
</table>

	Ra As	Ma	Mo
	D27:		
Sa	**Saptavim-**		
	-shamsha		
	(Strength)		
Me	Ke Ve Su		JuR

This chart is taken to demonstrate the role of debilitated and afflicted Sun as the cause of multiple diseases. Sun is Atma or soul. When Sun is weak in any divisional chart then the vitality of that division is lost. Here Sun is with Ketu and aspected by Saturn. The saving grace is cancellation of debilitation.

Her major problems surfaced in Venus Maha dasha. Problems in Venus dasha are given.

1. Respiratory problems in 1990 in Venus/ Venus.

2. Hip replacement in 1995.

3. Irregular heart beat in 1996 in Venus/ Rahu.

4. Brain tumour and seizure in 1997 in Venus/ Rahu.

5. Back injury in 1999 in Venus/ Jupiter.

Example Chest Cancer DOB 13 October 1958 TOB 7.30 POB Jaipur

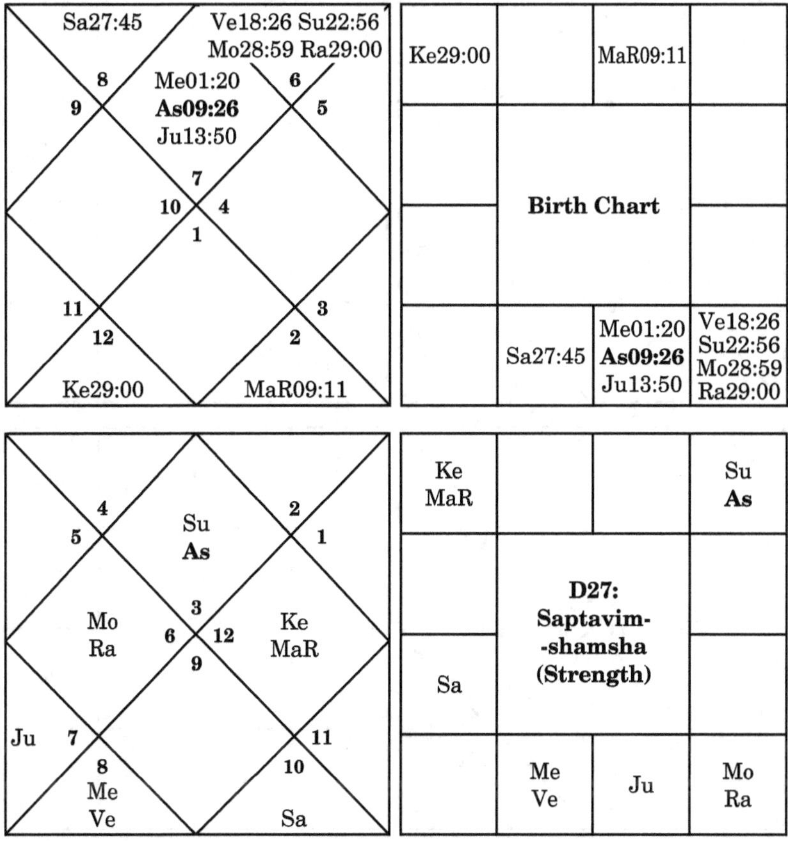

In D 27 Moon is with Rahu and aspected by afflicted Mars. Cancer is the sign under the influence of Saturn. Saturn is the strong eighth lord. Thus, Moon and its sign Cancer are the location of disease. This is representing chest. **When the sign and its lord both are under affliction then the common significations are important.**

He complained of chest pain in 1996. This was start of Saturn Maha dasha. Chest cancer was detected. Both Rahu and Saturn are causing disease. He died in 1998.

Example Ear DOB 1 January 1994 TOB 13.53 POB Delhi

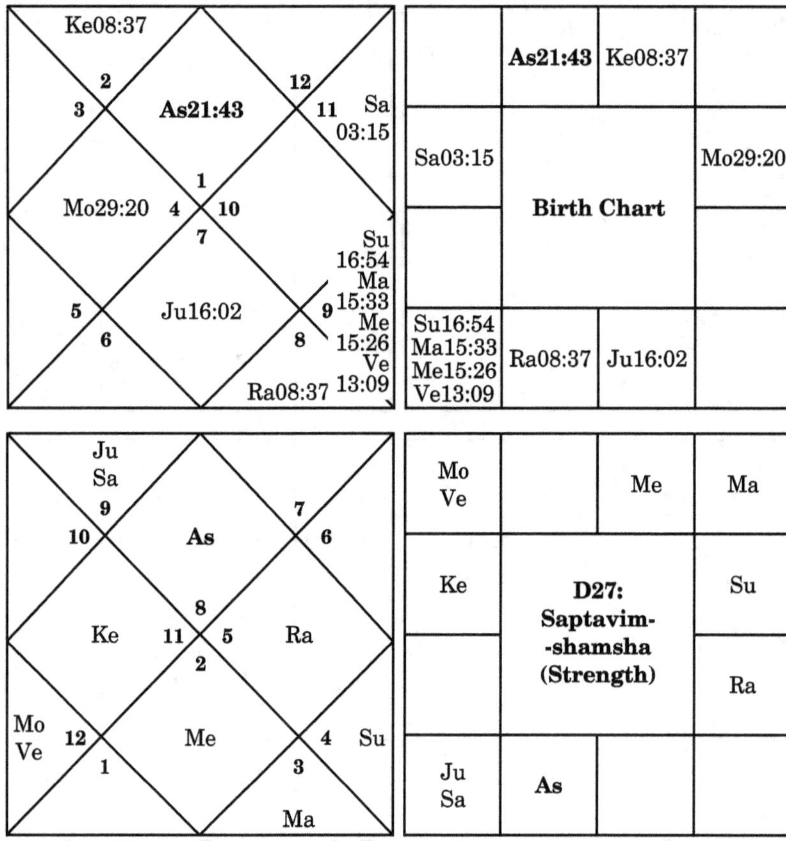

This child suffered from the age of 10 years. He developed a hole in his ears in 2003. In D 27 the afflicted planet is Jupiter. The signs under malefic influence are Gemini and Sagittarius. Gemini is eighth house in D 27 and sixth house in D 1. Gemini and Jupiter are significator of hearing and ears.

Jupiter is at 12 degrees in D 27 and gives internal disease.

Chapter 9

Remedies

Maharishi Parashar has suggested remedies to ward off evils and ensure good health. Two approaches have been suggested.

1. Propitiation of afflicting planets.

2. Propitiation according to Vimshottary dasha and antar dasha periods.

Normally the problem manifests in the dasha/ antar dasha of afflicting or afflicted planets. This is seen in birth chart and the other relevant chart. In this case it is D 27. Sometimes the problem comes in the dasha of afflicted planet. In these cases, propitiation is suggested for the afflicting planet so that the afflicted planet is relieved. **It is recommended that prayers to your Ishta Devata will be highly beneficial.**

Propitiation of afflicting planet

Let us understand the afflicting planet. We take an example and decide the afflicting planet.

Example DOB 29 March 1982, TOB 13.01, POB Upland CA USA

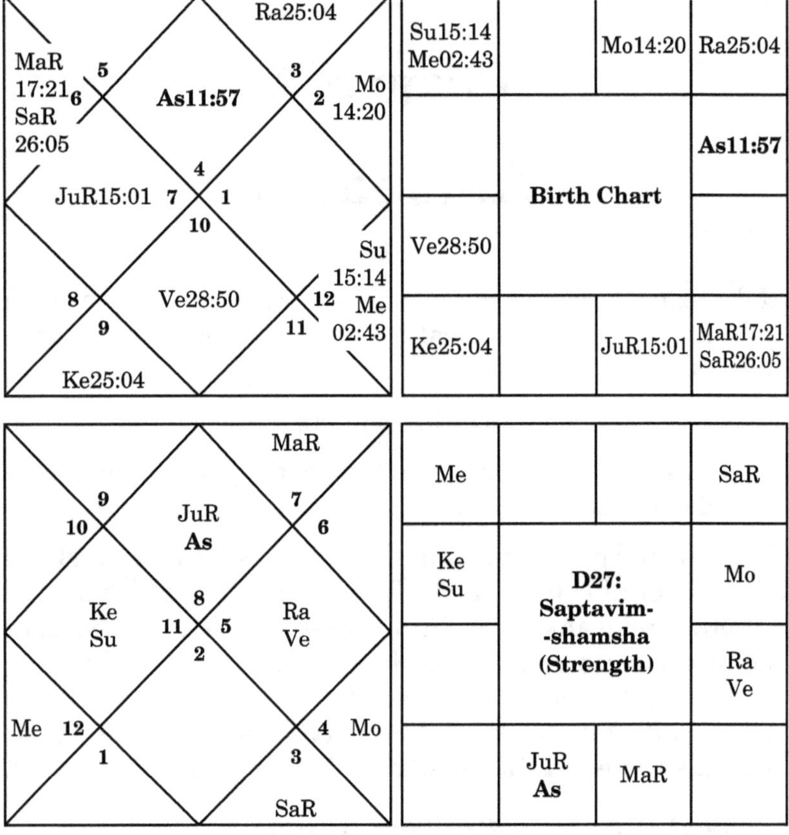

In D 1 Mercury is afflicted and is afflicted by Sun, Mars and Saturn. Dasha at birth was of Moon. The problem was at the time of birth.

In D 27 Venus is afflicted by Rahu, Saturn and Sun. Moon is in papa kartari. Which propitiation should be done? The nearest affliction is by Rahu and it is to be propitiated. For propitiation of Rahu, we check the sign lord of Rahu in D 30. It is in the sign of Venus and we should propitiate Venus.

SUN

Day	Sunday
Direction	East
Color	Red
Metal	Copper, gold
Flower	Lotus
Food	Rice cooked with jaggary
Grain	Wheat
Charity	Milking cow
Gem stone	Ruby
Japa mantra	"Aum Hrim Hrim Suriyaye Namah Aum"
Dhyan mantra	"Japa Kusuma Sankasham Kashyapeyam Mahadhyutim, Tamorim Sarva Papadhnam Prantoami Divakaram"

MOON

Day	Monday
Direction	North west
Color	White
Metal	Silver, bell metal, sphatika
Flower	Oleander
Food	Rice cooked in milk
Grain	Rice
Charity	Conch
Gem stone	Pearl
Japa mantra	Aum Sheer Putraay Vidmahe Amrit Tatvaay Dheemahi Tanno Chandra Prachodayat
Dhyan mantra	Dadhi Sankha Tusarapham Ksirodarnava Samphavam Namami Sasinam Somam Samphor MakutaBhusanam

MARS

Day	Tuesday
Direction	South
Color	Red
Metal	Copper, red sandal
Flower	Red Lilly
Food	Havishya
Grain	Tuvar
Charity	Bullock
Gem stone	Coral
Japa mantra	Aum Angarkaya Vidmahe Bhoomipalaya Deemahi Tanno Kujah Prachodayat
Dhyan mantra	Dharanigarbha Samphutam Vidut Kanti Samaprabham Kumaram Sakti Hastam Sa Mangalam Pranmam Yaham

MERCURY

Day	Wednesday
Direction	North
Color	Green like durva grass
Metal	Lead, gold
Flower	Lilly
Food	Paddy cooked in milk
Grain	Green gram
Charity	Gold
Gem stone	Emerald
Japa mantra	'Om Gajadhwajaaya Vidmahae Sukha Hastaaya Dheemahi Tanno Budha Prachodayaat'
Dhyan mantra	Priyangu Kalikas Yamam Rupena Pratymam Budham Saumyam Saumya Gunopetam Tam Budham Pranamamyaham

JUPITER

Day	Thursday
Direction	North east
Color	Yellow
Metal	Gold
Flower	White mulai
Food	Curd rice
Grain	Gram
Charity	Clothes
Gem stone	Yellow topaz
Japa mantra	Aum Guru Devaya Vidmahe Parabrahmane Dheemahi Tanno Guruh Prachodayat
Dhyan mantra	Devanamch Rsinamch Gurum Kanchan Sannibham, Buddhi Bhutam Trilokesham Tam Namami Brihaspatim

VENUS

Day	Friday
Direction	South east
Color	White or multicolored
Metal	Silver
Flower	Lotus
Food	Rice with ghee
Grain	Cow gram
Charity	Horse
Gem stone	Diamond
Japa mantra	Aum Rajadabaaya Vidmahe, Brigusuthaya Dheemahi, Tanno Shukrah Prachodayat
Dhyan mantra	Himkundmrinalabham Daetyanam Parabham Gurum, Sarvashastrapravaktaram Bhargavam Pranmamyaham

SATURN

Day	Saturday
Direction	West
Color	Blue
Metal	Iron
Flower	Shami
Food	Rice baked with sesame
Grain	Sesame seed
Charity	Black cow
Gem stone	Blue sapphire
Japa mantra	Aum Sanaischaraya Vidmahe, Sooryaputraya Dheemahi, Tanno Manda Prachodayat.
Dhyan mantra	Nilanjana Samabhasam Ravi Putram Yamagrajam Chaya Mrttanda Sambhutam Tam Namami Shanai Shwaram

RAHU

Direction	South west
Color	Dark honey
Metal	Lead
Flower	Malu
Food	Meat rice
Grain	Black gram
Charity	Iron
Gem stone	Gomed
Japa mantra	Aum Sookdantaya Vidmahe Ugraroopaya Dheemahi Tanno Rahu Prachodayat
Dhyan mantra	Ardhakayam Mahaviryam Candraditya Vimardanam Simkika Garbha Sambhutam Tam Rahu Pranmam Yaham

KETU

Direction	Southwest or northwest
Color	Brown, smoky
Metal	Brass
Flower	Red lily
Food	Rice cooked with pulses
Grain	Horse gram
Charity	Goat
Gem stone	Cat's eye
Japa mantra	Aum Chitravarnaya Vidhmahe, Sarparoopaya Dheemahi, Tanno Ketu Prachodayat
Dhyan mantra	Aum Palasa Puspa Samkasam Tarakagraha Mustakam, Raudram Raudratmakam Ghoram Tam Ketum Phanamam Yaham

The Navgraha Strotra is given for prayers to all nine planets.

॥ नवग्रह स्तोत्र ॥

अथ नवग्रह स्तोत्र ॥

श्री गणेशाय नमः ॥

जपाकुसुम संकाशं काश्यपेयं महद्द्युतिम् ।
तमोरिंसर्वपापघ्नं प्रणतौस्मि दिवाकरम् ॥ 1 ॥

दधिशंखतुषाराभं क्षीरोदार्णव संभवम् ।
नमामि शशिनं सोमं शंभोर्मुकुट भूषणम् ॥ 2 ॥

धरणीगर्भ संभूतं विद्युत्कांति समप्रभम् ।
कुमारं शक्तिहस्तं तं मंगलं प्रणाम्यहम् ॥ 3 ॥

प्रियंगुकलिकाश्यामं रुपेणाप्रतिमं बुधम् ।
सौम्यं सौम्यगुणोपेतं तं बुधं प्रणमाम्यहम् ॥ 4 ॥

देवानांच ऋषीनांच गुरुं कांचन सन्निभम् ।
बुद्धिभूतं त्रिलोकेशं तं नमामि बृहस्पतिम् ॥ 5 ॥

हिमकुंद मृणालाभं दैत्यानां परमं गुरुम् ।
सर्वशास्त्र प्रवक्तारं भार्गवं प्रणमाम्यहम् ॥ 6 ॥

नीलांजन समाभासं रविपुत्रं यमाग्रजम् ।

छायामार्तंड संभूतं तं नमामि शनैश्चरम् ॥ 7 ॥

अर्धकायं महावीर्य चंद्रादित्य विमर्दनम् ।

सिंहिकागर्भसंभूतं तं राहुं प्रणमाम्यहम् ॥ 8 ॥

पलाशपुष्पसंकाशं तारकाग्रह मस्तकम् ।

रौद्रंरौद्रात्मकं घोरं तं केतुं प्रणमाम्यहम ॥ 9 ॥

इति श्रीव्यासमुखोग्दीतम् यः पठेत् सुसमाहितः ।

Propitiation according to Vimshottari Dasha and Antardasha periods.

Sun/ Sun

1.   Undertake Mritunjaya Japa.

2.   Pray to Sun God.

Sun/ Moon

1.   Donate white cow and female buffalo.

Sun/ Mars

1.   Recite Vedic mantra and Mritunjaya Japa.

2.   Donate bull with proper rituals.

Sun/ Rahu

1.   Recite Durga Saptasanti or Durga Mantras.

2.   Donate goat

3.   Donation of black cow, female buffalo will subdue the bad effect.

Sun/ Jupiter

1.   Recite mantra of Ishta Devta.

2.   Donate gold and Kapila cow.

Sun/ Saturn

1.   Undertake Mritunjaya Japa.

2.   Donate goat, black cow or female buffalo.

Sun/ Mercury

1.   Recite Vishnu Sahastranam.

2.   Donate silver idol and grains.

Sun/ Ketu

1.   Recite Durga Mantras.

2.   Donate goat.

Sun/ Venus

1.   Undertake Mritunjaya Japa.

2.   Undertake Japa of Lord Shiva.

3.   Donate white cow and female buffalo.

Moon/ Moon

1.   Donate white cow and female buffalo.

Moon/ Mars

1.   Pay respect to Brahmins.

Moon/ Rahu

1.   Undertake Japa of Lord Shiva Mantra.

2.   Donate goat.

Moon/ Jupiter

1.   Recite Shiva Sahastranam.

2.   Donate gold in charity.

Moon/ Saturn

1.   Recite Mritunjaya or Kali Mantra.

2.   Donate cow or buffalo in charity.

Moon/ Mercury

1.   Recite Vishnu Sahastranam.

2.   Donate goat.

Moon/ Ketu

1.   Undertake Mritunjaya Mantra Japa.

Moon/ Venus

1.   Pray to Lord Shiva.

2.   Donate white cow or silver in charity.

Moon/ Sun

1.   Pray to Lord Shiva.

Mars/ Mars

1.   Worship Rudra to please Lord Shiva.

2.   Donate bull.

Mars/ Rahu

1.   Worship Naga Devta.

2.   Give food to Brahmins.

3.   Undertake Mritunjaya Mantra Japa.

Mars/ Jupiter

1.   Recite Shiva Sahastranam.

Mars/ Saturn

1.   Undertake Mritunjaya Mantra Japa.

Mars/ Mercury

1.   Recite Vishnu Sahastranam.

2.   Donate horses in charity.

Mars/ Ketu

1.   Undertake Mritunjaya Mantra Japa.

Mars/ Venus

1.   Donate cow and female buffalo.

Mars/ Sun

1.   Undertake religious worship.

Mars/ Moon

1.   Recite mantra of Goddess Durga or Laxmi.

2.   Donate white cow and female buffalo.

Rahu/ Rahu

1.   Undertake religious worship.

Rahu/ Jupiter

1.   Worship Lord Shiva.

2.   Donate gold idol in charity.

Rahu/ Saturn

1.   Donate black cow and female buffalo.

Rahu/ Mercury

1.   Recite Vishnu Sahastranam.

Rahu/ Ketu

1.   Donate goat in charity.

Rahu/ Venus

1.   Recite Mantra of Goddess Durga or Laxmi.

Rahu/ Sun

1.   Worship Sun God.

Rahu/ Moon

1.   Donate white cow and female buffalo.

Rahu/ Mars

1.   Give food in charity.

2.   Donate bull in charity.

Jupiter/ Jupiter

1.   Recite Shiva Sahastranam.

2.   Undertake Rudra pooja.

3.   Donate cow in charity.

Jupiter/ Saturn

1.   Recite Vishnu Sahastranam.

2.   Donate black cow and female buffalo.

Jupiter/ Mercury

1.   Recite Vishnu Sahastranam.

Jupiter/ Ketu

1.   Undertake Mritunjaya Mantra Japa.

2.   Donate goat in charity.

Jupiter/ Venus

1.   Donate white cow and female buffalo.

2.   Undertake pious deeds.

Jupiter/ Sun

1.   Perform Aditya Haridaya Patha.

Jupiter/ Moon

1.   Durga Saptasati Patha be performed.

Jupiter/ Mars

1.   Donate bull in charity.

Jupiter/ Rahu

1.   Undertake Mritunjaya Mantra Japa.

2.   Donate goat in charity.

Saturn/ Saturn

1.   Undertake Mritunjaya Mantra Japa.

Saturn/ Mercury

1.   Recite Vishnu Sahastranam.

2.   Give food grains in charity.

Saturn/ Ketu

1.   Donate goat in charity.

Saturn/ Venus

1.   Durga Saptasati Patha be performed.

2.   Donate white cow and female buffalo.

Saturn/ Sun

1.   Worship Sun God.

Saturn/ Moon

1.   Offer sesame seeds in fire as oblation.

2.   Give jaggery, ghee, rice mixed with curd in charity.

3.   Donate white cow and female buffalo.

Saturn/ Mars

1.   Perform Havan in fire.

2.   Give buffalo in charity.

Saturn/ Rahu

1.   Undertake Mritunjaya Mantra Japa.

2.   Donate goat in charity.

Saturn/ Jupiter

1.   Recite Shiva Sahastranam.

2.   Donate gold.

Mercury/ Mercury

1.   Recite Vishnu Sahastranam.

Mercury/ Ketu

1.   Donate goat in charity.

Mercury/ Venus

1.   Chant mantras of Goddess Jagdamba.

Mercury/ Sun

1.   Undertake Shanti Patha with proper rituals.

Mercury/ Moon

1.   Perform Japa of goddess Durga.

2.   Donate clothes in charity.

Mercury/ Mars

1.   Undertake Mritunjaya Mantra Japa to please lord Shiva.

2.   Donate cow in charity.

Mercury/ Rahu

1.   Perform Japa of Goddess Laxmi.

2.   Donate white cow or buffalo.

Mercury/ Jupiter

1.   Undertake Japa of Shiva Sahastranam.

2.   Give cow, land or gold in charity.

Mercury/ Saturn

1.   Undertake Mritunjaya Mantra Japa.

2.   Donate black cow or buffalo in charity.

Ketu/ Ketu

1.   Perform Japa of Goddess Durga and Mritunjaya Patha.

Ketu/ Venus

1.   Perform Japa of Goddess Durga.

2.   Donate white cow or buffalo in charity.

Ketu/ Sun

1.   Give gold and cow in charity.

Ketu/ Moon

1.   Please Moon.

Ketu/ Mars

1.   Give goat in charity.

Ketu/ Rahu

1.   Undertake Japa of Goddess Durga.

Ketu/ Jupiter

1.   Undertake japa of Shiva Sahastranam.

2.   Recite Mritunjaya Mantra.

Ketu/ Saturn

1.   Offer sesame seeds in fire as oblation.

2.   Donate black cow or female buffalo in charity.

Ketu/ Mercury

1.   Recite Vishnu Sahastranam.

Venus/ Venus

1.   Undertake Japa of Goddess Durga.

2.   Donate cow.

Venus/ Sun

1.   Worship Sun God.

Venus/ Moon

1.   Please Moon God.

Venus/ Mars

1.   Donate bull.

Venus/ Rahu

1.   Undertake Japa of Mritunjaya Mantra.

Venus/ Jupiter

1.   Undertake Japa of Maha Mritunjaya Mantra.

Venus/ Saturn

1.   Undertake Japa of Mritunjaya Mantra.

2.   Worship Goddess Durga.

Venus/ Mercury

1.   Recite Vishnu Sahastranam.

Venus/ Ketu

1.   Undertake Japa of Mritunjaya Mantra.

2.   Donate goat in charity.